Discoveri
Creative

M000303353

NEW WRITING VIEWPOINTS

Series Editor: Graeme Harper, *Oakland University, Rochester, USA*

Associate Editor: Dianne Donnelly, *University of South Florida, USA*

The overall aim of this series is to publish books which will ultimately inform teaching and research, but whose primary focus is on the analysis of creative writing practice and theory. There will also be books which deal directly with aspects of creative writing knowledge, with issues of genre, form and style, with the nature and experience of creativity, and with the learning of creative writing. They will all have in common a concern with excellence in application and in understanding, with creative writing practitioners and their work, and with informed analysis of creative writing as process as well as completed artefact.

All books in this series are externally peer-reviewed.

Full details of all the books in this series and of all our other publications can be found on http://www.multilingual-matters. com, or by writing to Multilingual Matters, St Nicholas House, 31-34 High Street, Bristol BS1 2AW, UK.

NEW WRITING VIEWPOINTS: 17

Discovering Creative Writing

Graeme Harper

MULTILINGUAL MATTERS
Bristol • Blue Ridge Summit

DOI https://doi.org/10.21832/HARPER8465
Library of Congress Cataloging in Publication Data
A catalog record for this book is available from the Library of Congress.
Names: Harper, Graeme, author.
Title: Discovering Creative Writing/Graeme Harper.
Description: Bristol; Blue Ridge Summit: Multilingual Matters, [2020] |
    Series: New Writing Viewpoints: 17 | Includes bibliographical references
    and index. | Summary: "This is a book about discovering how you do
    creative writing. How you begin, how you structure, how your writing
    process works, how a work embodies movement and change, what
    influences you, and, ultimately, how you end. The book is aimed at both
    students of creative writing and anyone wishing to begin, continue, or
    improve their writing"— Provided by publisher.
Identifiers: LCCN 2020002471 (print) | LCCN 2020002472 (ebook) |
    ISBN 9781788928465 (hardback) | ISBN 9781788928458 (paperback) |
    ISBN 9781788928472 (pdf) | ISBN 9781788928489 (epub) |
    ISBN 9781788928496 (kindle edition) Subjects: LCSH: Creative writing.
Classification: LCC PN187 .H366 2020 (print) | LCC PN187 (ebook) | DDC
    808/.02—dc23 LC record available at https://lccn.loc.gov/2020002471
LC ebook record available at https://lccn.loc.gov/2020002472

British Library Cataloguing in Publication Data
A catalogue entry for this book is available from the British Library.

ISBN-13: 978-1-78892-846-5 (hbk)
ISBN-13: 978-1-78892-845-8 (pbk)

Multilingual Matters
UK: St Nicholas House, 31-34 High Street, Bristol BS1 2AW, UK.
USA: NBN, Blue Ridge Summit, PA, USA.

Website: www.multilingual-matters.com
Twitter: Multi_Ling_Mat
Facebook: https://www.facebook.com/multilingualmatters
Blog: www.channelviewpublications.wordpress.com

The policy of Multilingual Matters/Channel View Publications is to use
papers that are natural, renewable and recyclable products, made from wood
grown in sustainable forests. In the manufacturing process of our books, and
to further support our policy, preference is given to printers that have FSC
and PEFC Chain of Custody certification. The FSC and/or PEFC logos will
appear on those books where full certification has been granted to the printer
concerned.

Typeset by Deanta Global Publishing Services, Chennai, India.

Contents

Acknowledgments

To Anna, and to Tommi, Sarah, Ellie, Laura and Flo at Multilingual Matters who have made working on this book, and all the others in the *New Writing Viewpoints* series, a true joy, both professionally and personally. Good wishes also to the newer members of the MLM team, Rose and Alice. Sincere thanks to each and all of you! To Dianne Donnelly, who as associate editor of the *New Writing Viewpoints* series, as well as a friend and colleague, has provided attentive insights, meaningful observations and occasional lighthearted speculations too! To the many students and colleagues around the world who engage in creative writing, both the practice of it and the critical examination of the practice and its results, my thanks for your shared discoveries and your continued enthusiasm. To my wife, Louise, and to our sons, Myles and Tyler, all my love, always.

Introduction

Discovering Creative Writing

We writers spend more time thinking about what is actually known about creative writing than anyone else spends thinking about that topic.

Of course, literary scholars clearly have a strong interest, though most often it is from the point of view of the text that has been produced, or in considering the background of the writer who produced that text, rather than from the point of view of doing the creative writing. Publishers also have an interest, wondering if readers will embrace a book, and perhaps about whether an author can write more than their first book, and whether each book will provide some profit and, occasionally, some additional form of recognition (win a prize, more generally contribute to the good reputation of the publisher, assist in attracting other authors and the building of a particular list).

Those in other creative industries – the media, performing arts, leisure software, music – no doubt ponder questions about the contributions of creative writers, who might write a script, a lyric, a scenario, and how good their contributions might be, and how those contributions relate to the other creative practices involved.

Historians, sociologists, educators – other groups wonder on the context of writing, or about who it is that different works represent, or about the social or economic conditions that prevail around the writer, or how creative writing might be used in literacy learning or in talking about events or observations in ways that allow those explorations to pique student interest and animate thoughts.

And yet, with all those interests, it is only we creative writers, faced with the prospect of writing something, and spurred on by a desire to do that job well, who are likely to regularly think about the extent of creative writing knowledge and the nature and application of creative writing knowledge to the task of writing. Virginia Woolf, such a regular, passionate and revealing diarist, writes this:

Wednesday 28 November (1928)

As for my next book, I am going to hold myself from writing till I have it impending in me; grown heavy in my mind like a ripe pear; pendant, gravid, asking to be cut or it will fall. The Moths still haunt me, coming, as they always do, unbidden, between tea & dinner, while L. plays the gramophone. I shape a page or two; & make myself stop. Indeed I am up against some difficulties. Fame to begin with. Orlando has done well. Now I could go on writing like that – the tug and suck are at me to do it. People say this is so spontaneous, so natural. And I would like to keep those qualities if I could without losing the others. But those qualities were largely the result of ignoring the others. They came of writing exteriorly; & if I dig, must I not lose them? And what is my own position toward the inner and the outer. (Bell, 1982: 209)

Woolf here navigating between the practicality of actually writing something, and deep, philosophic considerations about what she can write. Her writerly questions, just in this short passage, considerable: questions about success, spontaneity, quality, the shaping of a piece of writing, compositional strategies....

There are a number of disclosures we can make that usefully frame, and support, our own current and future discoveries about creative writing, ours as well as creative writing generally. These include:

Creative writing cannot happen without our actions – not a truism. Some creative forms, we could argue, exist in the world without human input. By this I mean, we acknowledge bird song, the way the sea shapes driftwood, the structures created in rock formations by the wind and rain. These analogues of our artistic practices remind us that beauty exists in the world but that some things we create do rely on our specific and distinctive human actions, and that we define such art according to the application of our human ingenuity and creativity. It is the application here that is important – creative writing involves human creativity *applied* to words.

A combination of imagination and intellect – creative writing has to be this combination because it involves the inventiveness, the originality of our imagination together with the structured, formal understanding of written language. This interaction and intersection of imagination and intellect power creative writing and it is through this powerful interplay of these two modes of understanding, these two tools, that we each engage with the writing arts.

Textual evidence tells only some of the story – some of the story, certainly, but not all. We can read final works – the novels, the poems, the short stories, the scripts – and consider their meaning, their social, individual, historical context, the genre they are, analyze their linguistic properties and explore the biographical and cultural background to their making. Canadian novelist, poet and essayist Margaret Atwood notes the material, textual evidence, but combines that note with the recognition that such textual writing evidence contains 'voice', that is beyond the page. She says:

> Surely that's partly because of the nature of writing – its apparent permanence, and the fact that it survives its own performance – unlike, for example, a dance recital. If the act of writing charts the process of thought, it's a process that leaves a trail, like a series of fossilized footprints. Other art forms can last and last – painting, sculpture, music but they do not survive as *voice*. And as I've said, writing is writing down, and what is written down is a score for voice, and what the voice most often does – even in the majority of short lyric poems – is tell, if not a story, at least a mini-story. Something unfurls, something reveals itself. (Atwood, 2002: 158)

We can seek out and examine the textual evidence that is created during creative writing – whether notes or emails or earlier drafts or diary entries, all kinds of textual material beyond those final 'permanent' texts that Atwood references. But, ultimately, creative writing happens because of your actions as a writer, and not all of those actions produce texts. Some actions occur in the moment of composition – ways we obtain information or how we speculate on an image or narrative point or character, what environmental factors are at play and how other people influence us or respond to our work, verbally, and our moods and changes in perspective and sense of purpose and passion for a project, or lack of it, and who we perceive as our audience. Not everything ends up as text, and to discover things about creative writing we need to recognize that and at the very least attempt to understand and interpret those non-textual activities.

Knowledge to be gained through the practice of doing it – as with all arts, there is an applied core to creative writing, things that are done and are learned fluidly as we work, that are developed in the situations we face when writing, that might not even be predictable before we are faced with them.

In some fields (education, for example, or sociology or anthropology) such knowledge is said to be observational or action based or comes from immersion in the practices of groups and communities, and its value is in direct engagement with human action (in this case, our actions as writers). These actions are fluid and interconnected, workings of our mind and imagination, and to endeavor to deal with this in ways that stop still what is happening, or divide up sections of it (for example, the texts produced divided from the environmental influences, those from the way we compose, daily life from the thoughts we're having and so on) falsifies what we are learning. Knowledge in practice and through practice is therefore about action and fluidity, seen accurately in motion and perceived in the doing.

Cultural conditions influence, across a spectrum – how we view genre and forms of creative writing, what is 'high cultural' and what is 'popular', who is the audience for what we write and why they are the audience – all this is culturally influenced. How we act as creative writers, and in what ways we perceive the value of what we are doing, and who supports what we do and how – this too is culturally influenced. Cultural influence is, of course, also seen in the subjects and the themes and the attitudes we depict in the works we produce. However, cultural influences are not restricted, and viewing these across a spectrum, taking into account also our individual psychology and the impact of our individual surroundings, education, personal circumstances, assists us in best understanding how creative writing happens, why it happens and in what ways it happens.

Methods of composing vary – creative writing is highly individualistic, meaning it incorporates creative independence, individualism and a good quantity of self-reliance. We can find some patterns of compositional behavior that are shared among us, such as the need of a writing tool, mostly limited to a small number of choices (for example, computer or pencil), and ideas about a practice we call 'drafting', which is widely represented as a method of writing. And the basic technical aspects of writing are often learned in shared, group educational environments. But, creative writing is individualized by the openness of the personal interaction between imagination and intellect, and by the activity of writing, which is most often done alone. 'When I turn my conscious mind to writing...', says Maya Angelou, whose first collection of poetry, *Just Give Me a Cool Drink of Water 'fore I Diiie* (1971), was nominated for a Pulitzer Prize:

> (my unconscious or subconscious is always busy recording images, phrases, sounds, colors, and scents). I follow a fairly rigid habit. I rise early, around 5.30 or 6 a.m., wash, pray, put on coffee, and arrange my mind in writing order. That is, I tell myself how lucky I am this morning is new, a day never seen before, that ideas will come to me which I have never consciously known. I have coffee and allow the work of the day before to flood my mind. The characters and situations take over the chambers of my existence until they are all I see and hear. Then I go to my writing room, most of the times a little cubicle I have rented in a cheap but clean hotel; rarely but sometimes it is a room in my own home. (Evans, 1985: 4)

How and where we find our preferred method of composing, and what it entails, is a subject of considerable significance if we are to learn all we can learn about creative writing.

What we gain – how we are satisfied by our creative writing might be approached by breaking this down into such main categories as (a) financial reward; (b) self-expression; (c) communication with others; (d) learning; (e) recording events, places and people; (f) empowering the imagination to reconsider or explore or extend beyond the observable into the perceivable. What we gain from creative writing, which might be a combination of these things and more, can reveal aspects of what we write, as well as why we write and, investigated further, offers us opportunities to consider our sense or senses of value in what we do. While a small percentage of creative writers worldwide are paid for writing, the larger number by far have other motivations or, at the very least, other points of personal satisfaction. What these gains entail, and indeed what we might consider 'losses' (for example, a failure to complete what we're working on, or a failure to win a writing competition, or a sense we haven't expressed ourselves well) enhance our understanding of what attracts us to creative writing.

Discovering Creative Writing is, in a manner, arranged in a linear fashion – starting with this introduction, 'Discovering Creative Writing', which sets out a framework for discoveries and summarizes the chapters in the book, concluding with 'Making Your Discoveries', which considers how you might use this information. However, none of us write creatively only in a linear way. Creative writing also works through our intersecting and interconnecting, imaginative leaps and inventive associations that are indirect and discontinuous.

In essence, while we do move forward as we write, we also move sideways and backwards, we layer and we insert, we overlay what is already written with what is newly being written. Therefore, the chapters in *Discovering Creative Writing* are arranged to emulate those actions, with the framework of 'Beginning' and 'Ending' intersected by explorations of the key writing components: 'Structures', 'Movements' and 'Influences'. Each chapter in *Discovering Creative Writing* is then further grounded around three focusing thoughts or concepts:

Why an area of investigation can give you information about creative writing, your creative writing, the writing of a particular project and creative writing in general.

What discoveries can be made, and what are the key aspects of those discoveries. What is the significance of these discoveries.

How we can use the discoveries we make.

Chapter 1: Beginnings

Creative writing discoveries can be found in origins, in the act of envisaging a work of creative writing – a novel, a poem, a video game script and ultimately starting out to write it. This starting out entails what is often called 'pre-writing' – what I have referred to elsewhere as 'foundation'.[1] This is the work of a creative writer even before the physical act of writing begins. Such starting out also involves the initial actions of inscribing – the first physical actions of writing. In this way, starting out is both practical (simple things like accessing a tool with which to write and finding the time) and conceptual (decisions about how to begin and, at least initially, what we are going to write).

In investigating beginnings, we can discover how we perceive an idea or in what ways a variety of influences spark our interests in a subject or theme. We can consider if structures seen elsewhere, say other forms of art, or in the natural world, in geography (for example, the contours of landscapes, or the mapping of roads and towns) or in mathematics (line lengths, number of pages), suggest the structural characteristics of what we are planning on composing. Beginning also often produces a combination of trepidation and excitement; the fact that it is so often up to the individual creative writer to turn the 'blank page' into a poem or a novel or a libretto, while at the same time this responsibility can also be seen as an opportunity, an adventure we initiate and we control. Beginning holds discoveries not only to what was (that is, what generated the project we are about to undertake), but also to what might become. The evidence of these things can be found in both the textual evidence (drafts, notes, correspondence, completed openings of works) and in the actions we take in order to start and when we start.

Chapter 2: The Structure of Your Work

Because creative writing involves inscription, and because written communication requires order and organization to be understood, we can discover in the structures of our creative writing – in the text and in the modes of writing we employ – evidence of our thinking, any processes we develop and our projecting of results.

Structure refers to the arrangement of things, to a constitution, a shape, a design, a layout, as well as to a relationship between components. Structure can also be used to describe an action – the act of *structuring* (that is, 'to structure'). In this sense, structuring can be part of the movement and flow of your composing, a specific element of the writing process. In structuring, we discover material evidence – written evidence and experiential evidence, meaning your actions and the influences on your actions as evidence.

Physical structures can be imagined or they can be right there in front of us. Either way, structures and structuring are taking the transcendental and making it concrete. If we look at the structures of our writing practice, sequences of action, relationships between kinds of actions, as well as the evidence found in our texts, our attempts, our final drafts, our discussions, we can see how we are giving solidity to our inventiveness. Structures can also be strategically evolved during your composing of a piece of creative writing. Structures can be expectedly unstable, and shift during composition, until you are satisfied they represent what you were aiming to communicate, and the aesthetic qualities you intended.

Chapter 3: Movement, Flow, Process

Everything in creative writing is movement. This is the case whether it is the simple but undeniable need for pen to move across paper, eye across screen, fingers across a keyboard, which is core for most writers to their composing. Or whether it is the movement forward and sideways, drawing in ideas and observations, things from right in our view and things from memory, creative writing is about motion. When a work is complete – or in some cases before that, as work-in-progress shared in a creative writing class or as a draft shared with a friend, editor, colleague – there is movement between the writer and their audience, an exchange that can influence the work at hand or future works we compose. There is also the movement through a writing life, the influences of time and culture that come about because of when we are and where we are. There is the movement from one work to another – some writers composing a single work at one time and other writers composing many works in staggered sequences, always writing more than one piece, moving between things. Discoveries to be made in movements relate to how we write, why we write and in what ways the compositional actions we undertake are a metaphor for the many other connective acts with which we are engaging.

Chapter 4: Knowing Your Influences

For example, much has been suggested about the influence of a particular writer on another writer. This is the case most often when these writers have been teacher-student, or when they have shared an environment (for example, writers in a particular part of a city or a writer associated with a particular publishing house or a particular editor). Writers have been interviewed about other writers they read, in an effort to track echoes and imitations in their work. Biographical and auto-biographical works about creative writers – most often those who have become well known – often explore the influence of a writer's location, education, family and friends.

Of course, biographical studies do this from the point of view of studying the writer as a subject, and autobiographical works are not mostly about the day-to-day practices of writing. For this reason, discovering the influences on your creative writing practice could well be present in the details of influence that no biographer would consider or be likely to find out and that an autobiographical study would be unlikely to greatly consider. Such writing influences as these could be summed up by the phrase 'knowing yourself'; however, the focus here is not merely a self-study in order to become more self-aware. In seeking specific information about how you approach writing creatively in order to better understand your actions and their results, the clues can be more pragmatic and usable.

In what ways does your personal background (family, friends, education, where you grew up) produce ways of thinking, ways of acting? Does such a background influence your themes and subjects and in what ways? How does what you have studied formally affect what you write about? What elements of the contemporary and the historical find their way into the style of your creative writing, the style of how you compose, your sense of your audiences?

When making a decision, you assess the value of the alternative decisions, you undertake analyses, consider the needs of the moment (that point in the screenplay or short story), perhaps relate those to the aims of the work as you perceive it when making the decision. Decisions are influenced not only by outside forces but also by your personal beliefs, your cognitive make-up, by your technical skills, by how much time you have to weigh up the options.

Seeking clues in your decision-making also allows you to consider the 'post-decision' conditions that prevail. And this can be the immediate impact – so that we can see during drafting a piece of creative writing that our decision to do something or incorporate something has obvious affect. Or why we shift directions or what goes into why we make changes. Or this can be impact in hindsight, so that we can consider the reasons why a completed work ended up the way it did. In some ways, this is not unlike the approach of a literary critic, considering a text according to how they read it personally, how they analyze what has brought it about, what theoretical position they apply to it; reading here being a creative activity of bringing the text into being all over again through their engagement with it. In other ways, our approach to decision-making, what it signifies and how it reveals itself is very unlike that of a literary critic because what we are seeking, as the creative writer writing the work or who has written the work, is pointers to the doing, indications of how and why we made the decisions we did.

Chapter 5: Endings

There is a well-worn comment, attributed in various forms to Leonardo da Vinci, French symbolist poet Paul Valéry and English novelist E.M. Forster, that a work of art (in this case, creative writing) is never completed, only abandoned. This comment seeks to explain why, even after releasing a work to an audience, an artist (in this case, a creative writer) might decide they would have done some things differently. This is not because all creative writers are inherently indecisive! Nor is it because we are easily and regularly dissatisfied. Rather, it is because creative writing takes many actions and has many potential results. Because of this, even when a work is 'complete', its many dimensions, the multiple actions that have taken place, choices brought together by your intellectual assessments and imaginative projections, challenge the idea of you being at a standstill. They unsettle your decision to stop responding to potential alternative approaches, potential alternative results.

Creativity involves newness, invention, innovation and originality. By preference, writing – other than creative writing – most often involves our attempts at certainty, at providing clear unequivocal communication, given that writing is designed to convey information and ideas and perceptions without us being present. As creative writers, we therefore navigate between ideals of creativity and the more common functions of the written word. How we conclude, and in what ways our completing a piece of work is a reflection of our sense of purpose, our aims and our objectives is an avenue of productive investigation (assisting us to discover these things). Such an investigation can also reflect on such things as available time and place for writing, formal deadlines provided to us by others and our impression of what we believe, aesthetically, narratively, in terms of points made or ideas explored or thoughts expressed or events described or impressions given, to be a finishing point.

Conclusion: Making Your Discoveries

To make accurate discoveries about our creative writing, we require proof about things we do and the results of what we do. To use that well-worn expression, that notion alone is surely 'not rocket science'? What we seek, if we are interested as writers in knowing more, is clear, accurate and usable information. The conclusions we reach can be tested in practice and considered in terms of the results we produce.

In essence, then, what we are seeking are clues. A clue is an indicator. A clue is potentially a guide to our actions. A clue informs our understanding. In exploring clues, we are determining how many avenues of investigation are available to us, and what potential they might have to offer us some new knowledge. Speaking of a clue is therefore shorthand for our intention of discovering pointers to how we write and what will be the results of us writing in that way. Clues could, in all expectation, lead to solutions to writing problems. They could be proof of how we think and how we feel, discovered in our actions or in the texts we produce or in how we interact with others (readers, publishers, friends).

Considering potential clues effectively provides a platform on which to consider both the linear aspects of creative writing – the starting out and moving to the conclusion of a project – and the non-linear aspects. The non-linear aspects include drawing from the past as well as the present, projecting a result into the future, engaging with our emotional needs as well as our intellectual ones, perhaps even moving between projects, one informing the others.

Acts of choice are fundamental in creative writing – they must be so because even though creativity suggests openness and invention, writing involves creating the comprehensible, the transferable, the exchangeable. Thus, from the very outset in choosing creative writing as your art form and mode of communication, you are choosing to take the creative and subject it to your decision-making.

Already we might consider that our decision-making processes include decisions about beginnings, structures, how the work will 'move', and about what we might control, in some way at least, in terms of the influence on our practice and outcomes. But what about the clues to the decision-making itself?

Decision-making involves assessing courses of action and making a final choice. In creative writing, that final choice might occur in several dimensions, and potentially recur in a number of iterations. Imagine the choice of idiom and how it might manifest itself throughout the composition of a poem, and in its ultimate released version. Imagine, similarly, how a decision to include an historical event in a novel influences not only the points of direct mention of the event but also how the work moves generally from the individual to the societal, the small aspects of individual lives to the larger aspects of nations or the world. Imagine the decision to write in between doing another job unconnected with creative writing – does that job influence what you write or how you write or who you envisage your audience might be?

Making your own discoveries about creative writing entails determining – personally, and particularly in relation to what you would like to know – **why** a particular area of investigation could give you the information you seek, **what** discoveries can be made and what their significance could be and **how** you can use discoveries you make to improve your own writing. *Discovering Creative Writing* takes the disclosures we can make that frame and support current and future discoveries about creative writing, and considers your particular, potential discoveries, along with the discoveries we can all make about creative writing, what it involves and what it truly is.

Note

(1) *Critical Approaches to Creative Writing*, Abington: Routledge, 2019, p. 70.

References

Atwood, M. (2002) *Negotiating with the Dead: A Writer on Writing*. Cambridge: Cambridge University Press.

Bell, A.O. (ed.) (1982) *The Diary of Virginia Woolf: Volume III: 1925–30*. Harmondsworth: Penguin.

Evans, M. (ed.) (1985) *Black Women Writers: Arguments and Interviews*. London: Pluto.

1 Beginnings

As a creative writer, you most likely answer the question of where you begin your work by simply drawing on observations and memory. That is, you locate the beginning of your writing at the point where you observe or remember you are/were physically doing it. In this vein, Joyce Carol Oates writes:

> As a younger child, pre-dating school, when I couldn't read or write, I'd compose 'books' in tablet form, dealing with adventures of awkwardly drawn chickens and cats with captions in flamboyant scrawls in mimicry of adult handwriting. (Maybe I'd imagine this was handwriting.) (Oates, 2003: 15)

So 'beginnings' in Oates's sense are in terms of beginning a writing life. More generally, you might recall such things as the place you were writing and the device you were using to write (computer, pencil or the like). You might remember you were seated, perhaps, recall the light in the room, the geographic location, any sounds, the time of day. To your mind therefore (and perhaps also to the minds of others), observably, demonstrably, you are/were working at some creative writing. Thus, as in the journals of André Gide, where he writes:

Saturday, 17 February (1912)

> I can only note in haste the rather whirlwind life of the last few days. I am writing seated on a bench in the Bois; the weather radiant this morning; this is the secret of my happiness. (Gide, 1984: 178)

Alternatively, or sometimes simultaneously, you might locate the beginning of your creative writing at the point where you decided you were going to write a poem, a short story, a play.... That decision clearly influenced certain actions that followed it. For example, perhaps you created a file on a laptop for the work you are doing, or bought a book you feel might assist what you are writing, or trawled the web looking for snippets of information, or walked outside to clear your head – all manner of actions brought about by the decision to write. This is how crime fiction writer Sara Paretsky remembers her decision-making:

> As for me, I wanted to write a crime novel. I wanted to create a woman who would turn the tables on the dominant views of women in fiction and in society. (Paretsky, 2007: 60)

Both your physical actions and the instance of decision-making do seem reasonable to suggest as the beginning of any creative writing. These are certainly supported by what is often called empirical evidence (observation) as well as by evidence of a cognitive process – that is, by your thinking (simply, you've given attention to something, applied some thought, perceived you'd like to do it and ultimately made the decision to do it). Our concern here is, of course, with the practical applications of such a suggestion – a discovery we can make that can be applied to your own writing, drawn from available clues, from the evidence and providing you with usable knowledge.

That said, beginnings have attracted some considerable philosophic investigation that gives us further food for thought on what exactly a beginning might be. Edward Said's *Beginnings: Intention and Method* explores beginnings in relation to the imagination, to action, to meaning and to invention. Admiring the work of Italian philosopher Vico (1668–1744), Said writes that one of Vico's contributions was that he showed

> the beginning in writing as inaugurating and subsequently maintaining another order of meaning from previous or already existing writing. (Said, 1975: 357)

So beginnings, according to Said's reading of Vico, inaugurate something and they maintain something. What then if where and how your creative writing begins, how it inaugurates and how it then maintains an idea, a viewpoint, a theme, is *neither* at the observable point of physical action *nor* at the point of decision-making?

What if – by examining the clues – we can confirm your creative writing did not begin when you physically began doing it, or when you first thought about doing it? What if, having discovered this, we can seek out information on when your creative writing actually began? And then, consider what impact that beginning has on your writing and on your writing results? What then?

What if the concept of 'beginnings' and the idea of 'a beginning' form part of your wider personal relationship with creative writing, and of your understanding of creative writing and of your general undertaking of creative writing? What then? What things, in that case, might you discover about creative writing and about your own practices of creative writing, which you can apply both to your practice and to your understanding of creative writing?

One way of investigating beginnings is to consider them as 'starting out' – literally, the initial point on a line of action. Such as in this jumping reference made by F. Scott Fitzgerald, suggesting jumping, forward, before stopping to review:

> Stories are best written in either one jump or three, according to length. The three-jump story should be done on three successive days, then a day or so for revise and off she goes. (Phillips, 1988: 38)

Author of Pulitzer Prize-winning novel *Pilgrim at Tinker Creek*, Annie Dillard even more directly references the notion of linearity when she writes:

> When you write you lay out a line of words. The line of words is a miner's pick, a wood carver's gouge, a surgeon's probe. You wield it, and it digs a path you follow. Soon you find yourself deep in new territory. Is it a dead end, or have you located the real subject? You will know tomorrow or this time next year. (Dillard, 1989: 3)

'Starting out' is also an expression we use when someone is new to something, a job or some other activity, an art practice ('she's just starting out as a landscape painter'), a sport, a leadership or management role ('she's starting out this week in the director's role'), and is used to refer to newness. Interestingly, it is also a descriptive expression used for a situation where someone has changed roles ('he started out as a pianist before he became a singer'). So 'starting out' can refer to a shift, to a re-positioning. It can even be used to suggest an unexpected success ('can you believe she started out as part-time designer and now she's leading the entire design team?'). Starting out additionally refers to intention, to objectives ('starting out as he means to continue') and to setting forth on an investigation or on a journey.

Considering how we 'start out' can be one way to consider how we begin. Generally, pointers to beginning in creative writing exist both in how we think and in how we act – remembering that clues can also be called indications or suggestions, solutions, proof, traces or pointers. Beginning can therefore be used to refer to:

Originating. The rule of thumb that no creative writing occurs unless it is undertaken is not as ridiculous as it sounds! To originate means to bring into existence. While we can consider where such originating occurs, and how it occurs, the significant thing here is that without originating, creative writing does not exist.

Consider how many things that you experience in the world are not originated. Rather, they are acquired or they are discovered. Consider if all your thoughts and all your ideas are originated – or, as is almost certain, are some of them acquired and others of them discovered? While in any of these cases the seeking out of something might be intentional, and therefore a form of origination, the acquiring and/or the discovery is not.

Creative writing is almost never about acquisition. And you do not discover your creative writing. Creative writing is also rarely fortuitous. The primary context of creative writing is that it is almost always intentional and that it is the result of your conscious actions. For these reasons, creative writing is about originating, about you actively bringing something into existence. In a lecture first delivered in 1985, American novelist John Barth declared:

> And so here we are, at the close of the twentieth century, some of us imagining it to be unimaginable at this hour of the world that the human literary/mythopoeic imagination can dream up yet another image with the profundity and staying power of those great predecessors – when for all we know, the thing might be being done next door, right now, by someone too busy doing it to attend these remarks of mine. (Barth, 1995: 63)

Traces of your influence as an originator can therefore be found in your ways of thinking and ways of acting. Indicators of this thinking and this action include:

• *Non-existence.* Your poem, computer game, sitcom, novel, short story did not exist previously. Why not? What proof is there, what indications of the reasons behind that work not previously existing?

You can often begin to understand your creative writing if you relate origination to your individuality. What contemporary influences are there on your personal originating? What traces of family or group influences – neighborhood, education, close relationships? What proof is there of your particular psychological or cultural influences that initiate and shape your origination? If, as sometimes is the case with screenwriting for example, more than one person is involved – a team of writers – your personal contribution to the collaborative enterprise is nevertheless discernible. Your impact on the logistics of the writing, your relationships with the other writers in the team, the subjects, the tone, the themes – all provide evidence and, at the very least, suggestions of where your influences occur.

Non-existence means you are making something where there was nothing. In his well-known essay, 'The Ontology of the Sentence or How to Make a World of Words', novelist, short-story writer and philosopher William Gass begins:

> It might at first seem difficult – to make a world of words – but actually nothing is easier. Think how Plato's Demiurge did it, or the Muse of Lucretius … not needing a syllable, only a little open space, a length or two of line, and perhaps a gentle push. We must try to be brave. (Gass, 1976: 308)

Considering the reason for the non-existence is one way of understanding your starting out, and the ways you begin to form a piece of creative writing, and your role in doing that. Your personality, background and historical and current social cultural influence – all these leave traces in your writing practice as well as in the results of that practice.

• *Conceiving*. To conceive has several meanings, including 'to produce a plan'. A plan for your creative writing might be loosely defined or it might be intricately developed. Both a physical plan, or lack of one, and the time taken on planning are relevant here because some writers plan extensively and some seemingly not much at all. However, even those writers who appear not to plan conceive of what they are attempting. Very simply, they plan in some fashion to complete something. To conceive can, of course, also relate to imagining or reasoning. This means, both literally and figuratively, that you 'have something in mind'. Conceiving involves having an opinion, possessing a viewpoint that you wish to present. That in itself is often a strong motivation for your creative writing – you have something you feel you want to say.

Conceiving is a word also widely used to refer to becoming pregnant. It therefore naturally relates to an expectation of childbirth. Colloquially, it is telling that a figurative reference to 'giving birth' is regularly used by creative writers when discussing one or other of their creative writing projects. This widely shared quote from Flannery O'Connor captures both the reference and the more common use of it, relating to the idea of creative writing being something involving much effort:

> Writing is like giving birth to a piano sideways. Anyone who perseveres is either talented or nuts. (Magee, 1987: 13)

And here too from Ralph Fletcher, relating the childbirth metaphor to the teaching of writing:

> I learned an important idea about teaching writing while preparing for the birth of my son. In our childbirth class, our teacher had this suggestion for husbands (and writing teachers) who are nervous about doing and saying the right thing at the critical moment. Relax, she told us. Try to remember that *tenderness is more important than technique*. (Fletcher, 1993: 18)

Anthropomorphizing tendencies aside, the fact that the colloquial reference to conceiving and ultimately giving birth has both physical and emotional elements tells us something about the way in which we perceive our writerly activities. Creative writing is never far from feeling, and it is dependent on origination – the bringing into being that is clearly the focus of conceiving, pregnancy and childbirth.

• *Originate meets originality*. We often discuss creativity in relation to inventiveness and innovation, newness and the imagination. We also relate creativity to originality. As their appearance suggests, origination and originality share an etymological history. Notions of originality are influenced by their cultural origin. Originality is not considered in the same way in every culture or valued in the same way in every culture. Because you are bringing something into existence, you are also using your imagination as a constructive tool. That is the general meaning of origination. It is entirely possible for your imagination to provide you with (perhaps) enjoyable diversions from day-to-day life, with (perhaps) frightening or pleasing scenarios based on projecting events or objects that are not in front of you into your mind, with (perhaps) fantastical versions of our world or other worlds, our lives or entirely other lives. But when we originate creative writing, we construct something that is physically present; throughout, you make your imagination a construction tool, so that what you see in your mind becomes something present as inscribed words. Novelist and literary critic, John Gardner, uses what we can call 'constructive references' in this paragraph on the imagination:

> Art depends heavily on feeling, intuition and taste. It is feeling, not some rule, that tells the abstract painter to put his yellow here and there, not there, and may later tell him that it should have been brown or purple or pea-green. It's the feeling that makes the composer break surprisingly from his key, feeling that gives the writer the rhythms of his sentences, the pattern of rise and fall in his episodes, the proportions of alternating elements, so that dialogue goes on only so long before a shift to description or narrative summary or some physical action.....
> He knows when and where to think up and spring surprises,

those startling leaps of the imagination that characterize all of the very greatest writing. (Gardner, 1991: 7)

Introducing, opening, commencing. These, as actions and as concepts, offer us further assistance in how to understand and employ ideas about beginnings in creative writing. If we think of beginning in these terms, we recognize not only that completed pieces of creative writing have what are most often called 'introductions'; but, even more significantly, that much of what we do in creative writing involves some kind of introducing, opening or commencing.

• *Introducing* can refer to put into use, to begin to apply, to bring into a situation, to present or to announce. Introducing therefore always takes the passive and makes it active, the invisible and makes it visible. If we think of how we can do that, in writing, we begin to see how we might develop a practice of creating openings of works, beginnings of works of creative writing. Introducing can also mean to present something or someone by name. So, to introduce is to give a name to something, make it tangible. Naming enters something into both our material and mental worlds. So, in that case, starting out involves identifying something in order to incorporate it.

• *Opening.* This is often used as a synonym for 'beginning'. We see its literal use more in relation to performances than in relation to written texts: 'at the opening of the play', 'at the opening of the film'. Performances and films also have 'opening nights' – the ephemeral nature of the performance/screening suggesting that what happens there and then has a singularity about it. After 'opening night', the performances might indeed be similar but not identical to the inaugural event, which has a uniqueness about it by being the first of its kind (or so it is suggested).

A book's 'opening' tends to be referred to more figuratively, so that the first few pages, the initial chapter, takes on the patina of a performance, suggesting what is ahead might interest and entertain, inform or enlighten, and that you have entered into that work.

Traditionally, a book also had to be 'opened' in order to be experienced. Certainly, there are variations on those particular mechanics, not least there are contemporary variations based on the nature of electronic texts; but, most often, a paper book has involved some kind of action to open it – and thus we have expressions such as 'he's an open book' or 'open the book' (which refers to revealing secrets). Starting out, in the guise of opening, therefore has both literal and figurative meaning – and it attaches itself to notions of beginning that contrast a lack of access (closed) to the granting of access (open). As a creative writer, when you start out, when you open, you give the reader or audience access.

• *Commencing* makes starting out not a prelude, but rather a first step in a process or an operation, suggesting an ongoing sequence or repetition of things. To commence is to start something that will therefore continue.

As a creative writer, this notion of commencing is useful in determining what aspects you can present that will have a longer-term purpose, repeated in some resonant way, referenced later or recalled in alternative ways. Commencing is, in this sense, also continuing. In fact, if someone were to say 'she commenced running, and then stopped', our response would likely be to wonder why she stopped or what stopped her. In other words, to commence is a starting out that suggests some longevity, some sense of continued purpose.

To commence is therefore to set forth, to set out, to look forward and to move forward. This kind of starting out has an implied, even sometimes an explicit means of propulsion. Implied when a creative writer makes no particular reference to what lies ahead in their work but the simple size of the physical object (the poem, the book, the script) suggests you will need to be propelled through it, and explicit when a creative writer uses references to events, characters, places, that have not yet been revealed.

The words you use, the way you structure your writing, the lines, the sentences, the use of tense and references to time are dynamic forces. To commence is to start that dynamism, that writerly means of propelling things forward. This is the case whether through suggesting what might be seen ahead, or implying what questions might be answered. Or pointing to something to be approached (looking to the future or the past, using the dynamics of time). Or producing a sequencing of movements that suggests a continuation by creating a rhythm, a pace that is compelling for the reader as much as it is impelling for the text you're creating.

In this sense, commencing is the idea of beginning used by the creative writer as an engine to create this movement; and that movement, however small it might be at first, however slight, draws the attention of the reader or audience. In that further sense, this movement can be as subtle yet piquing as something caught out of the corner of the reader's eye or as bold and direct as the thrust of an aircraft taking off with the reader on board. Short-story writer, memoirist and novelist Tobias Wolff shows something of that dynamism in his reply to interviewer Jay Woodruff, who asks: 'Do you always have to be sure you've found the right first sentence in order to find the rest of the story?':

> TW: I simply need a place to begin. Later on, when I revise, I often think of a better first line, especially, of course, if I've decided to change point of view, as I did in this story. Once in a while I'm lucky enough the right first sentence in the very beginning.... I try to be as open to chance as possible when I'm writing. If I have things too firmly in mind I lose a certain fluidity and ability to be surprised, which is very important to me. (Woodruff, 1993: 26)

So, fluidity, chance, changes... such are Wolff's dynamic notions, the impetus that is 'very important' to him.

When considered as beginning, **establishing** is an alternative to commencing.

In the establishing sense of beginning, rather than the engine, the propulsion-like approach associated with commencing, beginning is instead a grounding. That is, to establish is to lay the foundations or to put something in place.

Establishing is thus beginning by setting out. When we see beginning this way, you as a creative writer are aiming to offer a platform on which other things can be successfully built. More so, in fact, the suggestion is not that they *can* be built; but, rather, that they *will* be built. This is a reader or audience expectation – that you, establishing some sense of what things are, where things are, who is involved, what is being suggested, how what is written (or, in your case, being written) forms the basis of some ongoing commitment. You, as the writer, are offering an experience to the reader, and it is an experience to be based on what you are setting out. This is not to say you cannot shift the basis or condition or form of what you establish, but establishment is one aspect of beginning, and initiating a writer–reader relationship. Walter Besant alludes to this relationship in his lecture, *The Art of Fiction*, remarking:

> Of course, what the author cannot set down, the reader cannot understand. (Besant, 1885: 26)

Poet Donald Hall adds the transient element, the potential for shifting, when he says:

> Many poems begin for me without any sense of where they will go; then the voyage of revision is pure discovery. (Woodruff, 1993: 232)

Beginning approached as establishing can offer a heightened opportunity for complicating the action. You can unsettle expectations with alternative or questionable points of view. Change tone or timbre, rhythm or viewpoint. Content can warp or morph into alternative or contrasting elements or sources of information.

To begin by establishing, to start out by laying down a foundation, is much like it is in the architectural sense. While establishing suggests a footprint, a potential size and shape, it can indeed be that as a creative writer you challenge expectations, unsettle what you have laid down, making your beginning an opportunity to connote, allude. The laying down offers the reader a later opportunity to realize that you had given them the tools to understand, and connect to the idea, story or theme right from the start.

Creating. Quite naturally, beginning viewed as creating is immediately familiar to us, as creative writers. We generally perceive this to be what we are doing – beginning to create! Our kind of writing is, by definition, empowered by our inventiveness, our imagination, our originality. Therefore, no matter how much we might recognize and acknowledge influences beyond ourselves, it is to our individual creativity we most often turn when we seek to define what we do. That said, some writers view the real creating as beginning some time after they have begun to write. Peruvian Nobel prize-winning novelist, essayist and playwright Mario Vargas Llosa says this:

> Creation really begins for me when I have a first version of the novel, when I have to choose, to select, to eliminate everything that is not worthwhile for the story. When I discover that within this magma there are logical and coherent trajectories and some forces, or drives, in the characters that must be followed and used, I begin to feel that I am in the process of literary creation, of inventing something. (Llosa, 1991: 46)

In the sense of an identity linked to creating and to the cultural recognition of artists, it is natural that those of us working in the literary arts would consider beginning from the viewpoint of creating – and in doing so, making that notion of beginning one of engaging our imagination.

Beginning seen as the engagement of our imagination, makes beginning the point at which the mechanical aspect of writing, the intellectual aspects of analyzing or critically considering ideas, events and observations first meet the imaginative conjectures creative writing entails, the speculations, the rearranging or mixing of influences, the fantastical leaps, the mental representations of things or events not present. We can call this kind of beginning the *consolidating moment*. That is, the consolidation of the imagination and the intellect that is needed to write creatively.

With writing a system of signs and symbols requiring systemic understanding and the use of identifiable formal characteristics, and the imagination having less restraint, potentially being more free-flowing, more ingenious, more generative, the consolidation of imagination and intellect through writing is the defining moment. The decision to write creatively is thus the beginning of a way of engaging with observation or feeling or ideas or emotions – either in the making of a single piece of work or, indeed, as a guiding way of approaching much of your writing.

Finally, beginning can be viewed as *initiation*. To use an analogous context: when someone is first introduced to a practice, or a group, or even to a situation that involves challenging activities ('today was his initiation into the world of rock climbing'), they are said to be 'initiated'. Initiation is certainly a starting out for the person involved – in the case of your creative writing both the audience (the reader is initiated into the world of the poem or the novel or the play) and you, in the sense that your initiation involves immersion, more or less, into the work that you are creating. Initiating, taken as beginning, entails some sense of being an outsider invited in, of attempting something new, of learning. Novelist and short-story writer Cynthia Ozick speaks of initiation when she recalls first writing a play:

> There is plenty for the uninitiated playwright to learn from the living air of a reading, a rehearsal, a developing performance in the theater itself; and from an actor's cadence or lift of the eyelid; and from an impassioned talk with a seasoned playwright (and no one is more generous than lifelong playwrights, who are a band of mutually sympathizing cousins); and above all from a trusted and trusting director who recognizes the writer as writer. (Arana, 2003: 255–256)

In Ozick's sense, both the writer (entering a new project, coming to understand it) and the reader (most often encountering the finished work, not the work in progress) are learning. Beginning writing, and beginnings (openings, first lines, first chapters, first scenes) therefore are about a specific kind of literacy – what does the work mean, how does it mean it, who is it for, what are its intentions, how does it relate to what I already know…? Initiation here as guidance and preparation and direction.

In order to make some usable discoveries, consider your starting out strategies, your sense of beginning. In fact, consider if you currently have strategies at all – or, rather, is much that you do the result of fortuitous circumstance, simply putting 'pen to paper', and would not in any sense be something you would call a concerted strategy.

Of course, you might decide beginning that way is itself a strategy! In the same vein, you may map out things you commonly do (or, if you haven't yet done them, that you believe you would do) to begin a particular project. Consider the impact such beginning strategies might have. For example, if you wrote in a certain place, spent a certain amount of time on research before writing, interviewed someone, read around various books that might inspire you, tried some spontaneous writing experiments…. What might your approach to beginnings do in terms of your goals? Consider preparation – the concept of it, and the kinds of things you'd label as being preparation.

Similarly, comparing beginnings – the material manifestation of opening a poem, or a novel, a play, a script – and what these do in the realm of origination, introduction, initiation, for example. Here, structural characteristics of beginning meet thematic, subject characteristics. Here too, there is an opportunity to compare the range of what is established and the ways in which a trajectory is indicated for what comes next. If, as creative writers, we examine both our actions in beginning and the textual evidence of beginnings, in conjunction, we have the clearest sense of what we personally conceive as starting out, the value we place on certain actions, communications and impressions. We're looking here at what is initial and what underpins what comes next. And we are providing a comparative foundation too for what changes, what evolves, what is discovered while writing.

References

Arana, M. (2003) *The Writing Life: Writers on How They Think and Work.* New York: Public Affairs.

Barth, J. (1995) *Further Fridays: Essays, Lectures and Other Non-Fiction, 1984–1994.* Boston, MA: Little Brown.Besant. W. (1885) *The Art of Fiction.* Boston, MA: Cupples, Upham and Co.

Dillard, A. (1989) *The Writing Life.* New York: Harper and Row.

Fletcher, R. (1993) *What a Writer Needs.* Portsmouth, NH: Heinemann.

Gardner, J. (1991) *The Art of Fiction: Notes on Craft for Young Writers.* New York: Vintage.

Gass, W. (1979) *The World Within the Word.* New York: Basic.

Gide, A. (1984) *The Journals of Andre Gidé 1889–1949.* London: Penguin.

Llosa, M.V. (1991) *A Writer's Reality.* London: Faber.

Magee, R.M. (ed.) (1987) *Conversations with Flannery O'Connor*. Jackson, MS: University Press of Mississippi.

Oates, J.C. (2003) The importance of childhood. In M. Arana (ed.) *The Writing Life: Writers on How They Think and Work* (p. 12). Cambridge MA: Public Affairs.

Paretsky, S. (2007) *Writing in an Age of Silence*. London: Verso.

Phillips, L. (1988) *F. Scott Fitzgerald on Writing*. London: Equation.

Said, E. (1975) *Beginnings; Intentions and Meanings*. New York: Columbia University Press.

Woodruff, J. (1993) *A Piece of Work: Five Writers Discuss Their Revisions*. Iowa City, IA: University of Iowa.

2 The Structure of Your Work

Powered by your imagination, creative writing is sometimes thought to be an exuberant endeavor where your originality takes ordinary writing and does unusual things with it. While this occasionally might be true, much more often creative writing is a form of writing in which standard rules of written communication prevail and, as a creative writer, you imbue these with imaginative intention, creative insights, inventive suggestions.

Discovering more about structure allows us (who very likely will not be present when our written work is received by others) to consider how structure is both a writing trait and a writing tool. As a trait, structure can be considered a specific characteristic of creative writing – indicating ordering and the relationships between one thing and another, one event and another, showing a juxtaposition or a contrast, providing direction and suggestions on how we should interpret what we are offered.

A trait is a distinguishing quality, so structure can indeed identify what a piece of creative writing happens to be, and even who wrote the piece. Structure can also differentiate the period in which a piece was written, or where it was written. Structure can additionally reference other things – natural structures, mathematical models, for example – or relate to general laws that inform a work of creative writing (so, for example, a suggested general law that 'human progress comes about through single-minded determination' could produce a work of simple sentences and brief descriptions). In their book, *On Story: Screenwriters and Their Craft*, Barbara Morgan and Maya Perez quote numerous instances of writers giving form to a work:

From *Dog Day Afternoon* (1975) screenwriter Frank Pierson: 'I've been writing for many years and discovered that it's no easier now than when I started. Structure is everything' (Morgan & Perez, 2013: 63).

From *Bicentennial Man* (1999) screenwriter Nicholas Kazan: 'You don't have to structure as Syd Field does or as any of us do. You can structure your own way as long as you are sustaining mystery and the audience is compelled to continue to watch. You have some form of narrative structure, and that's all you need' (Morgan & Perez, 2013: 63).

Structure is also a writing tool, a specific element of the movement and flow of your writing, a component of process. It can (a) be used to give your task of writing a form, allowing you to anchor progress to it, reminding you that you have almost completed a chapter or created a requisite number of lines or offered enough changes of scene to lead the film viewer to consider where your film might go next. And it can (b) be considered in the perhaps mundane, but nevertheless constructive way of 'working time', the structure of your writing life. So, rather than a randomly undertaken, perhaps never-quite-done activity, your creative writing is a set of actions with a time and a place and, perhaps even an end goal for each writing session. In relation to *both*, of the structuring of a work and the structuring of a life as a writer, French writer and philosopher Jean-Paul Sartre recalls this entwined relationship:

My plots became more complex; I introduced a wide variety of incidents, pouring everything I read, good and bad, haphazardly into these hold-alls. The stories suffered; yet there was a gain: I had to invent linking passages and I immediately became a little less of a plagiarist. And then I divided myself in half. The previous year, when I was 'making films', I was acting myself, flinging myself whole-heartedly into the world of imagination, and convinced more than once that I was completely engulfed in it. As an author, I was still the hero: I projected my epic dreams through him. Yet there were two of us: he did not bear my name and I referred to him only in the third person. (Sartre, 1971: 93)

Structure, in the general sense, refers to the arrangement of things, to a shape, a design, a layout, to the constitution of something, as well as to a relationship between components. For example, the structure of a house might indeed include how many bedrooms and bathrooms it has, whether it is one story or more, where the kitchen is located, as well as its exterior design, its relationship with the yard around it, how it is situated, how many doors lead into it, how these relate to the movement through the house, what this movement happens to be and how it is encouraged. Structure can also be used to describe an action, such as in the statement: 'she set out to structure the day so she could be at the library before 5.00 pm'. In the case of creative writing, both noun and verb, thing and action, are used, and how they are used and in what ways that use is relevant to our personal investigating of creative writing.

Because structure (the thing) at some point leaves us and becomes one indication to our readers or audiences of what we think and mean, it can be that structure (the thing) represents us in some way or ways, that it is imbued with the characteristics we believe best convey our intentions. Structure (the action) entails technical choices and the application of writing conventions, or the challenging of these, and the consideration of alternatives (as much as we at any point know the full range of alternatives available to us) and the mechanics of taking a vision of a structure and getting it 'onto the page'.

Macro and Micro Structures

As the natural world shows us, structures include structures within them. From the atom to the universe, structures contain other structures and have relationships within those structures, as well as with structures that exist outside of them. We can consider the macrocosm and microcosm of structures in ways such as these, specifically in relation to creative writing:

• *What is within what?* The simplest creative writing examples are perhaps chapters within novels or stanzas within poems, acts within plays, scenes within acts. What is within what also assists to consider what is outside of what. So, we recognize that a certain chapter in a novel contains exposition (presented as summary) that sets up the protagonist's back-story. We know the next chapter contains a scene in which there is an exchange of dialogue between the protagonist and some less significant characters, that reveals something of how the backstory impacts on the protagonist's way of thinking. The summary and the scene are embedded in different chapters, but they also relate, and produce meaning, *across* chapters. Philip Stevick, writing of the chaptering techniques of Laurence Sterne and George Eliot, observes:

> At the end of *Middlemarch*, George Eliot suggests that every end is also a beginning. Sterne does her one better. What his manipulation of chapters does is to suggest a distrust of chapters, more than a recognition of beginnings in ends, a denial of the reality of the narrative unit. Time after time, what looks like an episode is no episode, what looks like a digression is no digression. What such an internal, associationist, apparently capricious organization is precisely a radical reorientation of the configural mechanism, which is possible in fiction. (Stevick, 1970: 30)

Structures contain, but structures also communicate – with one another and between one and others or between some and many. The opening lines of a poem might well set up not only a tonal quality, a subject, a theme, but also a resonant structural signal that reminds the reader, on its return, once, twice, many times, of the opening thought, the initial revelation. Structures build on other structures, within them – so we might have an establishing scene in a film script from which future scenes emerge, each relating back to the establishing scene and taking from it to offer sub-structures. So, we enter a street setting in which there are three characters, and the scene is written to allow each to speak – those visual and oral reference points provide an interlinked structure to future scenes. Similarly, a novel can involve multiple viewpoints and sections in it might be structured so that the same or connected events are revisited, juxtaposed or contrasted to raise questions about the validity of one or other character's interpretations.

Structure can also provide an indicator for what lies out-side the dimensions of a work – an excerpt from the popular press or an historic line-drawing or a sequence involving diary entries (fictional though these might be) or 'found' letters could equally say 'there are echoes of what you are reading that live beyond this text' and 'this work of creative writing is situated within certain parameters'. Structure can establish the integrity of a work, where its borders lie and why (because of the poem's viewpoint, or the limited knowledge of a story's narrator), and in doing so it can establish and promote the text's identity, and thus how we recognize it.

• *How does the smaller relate to the larger, and vice versa?* A question of interaction, interrelation, between structural components. Do these work so that the larger *encompasses* the smaller? Imagine, say, a libretto for an opera where the rhyme scheme incorporates smaller, echoic rhyme schemes that add to the dramatic effect of the piece. Or are the smaller components like bricks put together until the entire construction is com-plete? Here, imagine a short story composed of seven sections and each section progresses the story and each contributes in some way to the overall result. Or is the larger structure not so much made up of smaller components but is more the aspect of things that ensures all the smaller elements have a purpose, make some sense, can exist in the first place? So, say a screen-play set during a war which uses that setting and that condition to frame every action and character action within the piece. These structural relationships come about through your writ-erly way of thinking as much as through the graphic appearance of the texts you produce. In other words, though 'small' and 'large' suggest something you might see or imagine, in terms of volume or quantity, the structural shapes and relationships here are not only graphic ones but also conceptual ones. They relate to such things as their importance or their role in the explora-tion of a subject or theme or their importance in the depiction of a character or viewpoint or emotional context.

• *What defines the larger structures?* These could be seen as frameworks or viewed as the containers of action or observa-tions, or mechanisms in which there are smaller mechanisms.

How you view them will impact on how you write them, the roles those larger structures take in your overall structuring of a work. In thinking on this, a larger structure might refer to the spread of time covered in a work, or the pattern of rises and falls in action, or an organizational scheme based on presenting contrasting images or viewpoints or tones, or a metaphor that unfolds as the work progresses or on cause and effect. Poet, playwright, translator and novelist D.M. Thomas, speaking about his process in writing *The White Hotel*, says this:

> I was hopeful of *The White Hotel*. I thought it could become the best thing I'd written, and might pay the mortgage for a year or two.... The prose-fantasy had been dream-written almost; with the Freudian analysis I would have to apply concentrated logical thought. And I knew next to nothing about Freudian theory... (Thomas, 1988: 46)

The material by Freud, about Freud is serving both as subject and structuring guide for Thomas. It is the larger structure of a novel that suggests the smaller structures, fiction to be entwined with fact, fictional characters with real figures, to create what is ultimately a chronicle that explores the relationship between the inner life of someone and the outer life of culture, the world.

• *What defines the smaller structures?* Are these simply components – to continue the mechanism metaphor, are they therefore cog-like elements in a machine? Or are they building blocks? Or are they the nails that hold together the entire structure? Small in size is perhaps one thing – a paragraph, a stanza, a film scene with its sluglines – but the micro structures of a work of creative writing are where nuance occurs, resonance, which are sizable writing devices, influential ones in any work.

• *What are the design characteristics, the arrangements that involve the macro and the micro?* Beyond definition, those ways in which structures are perceived, there are the combinatory characteristics, the patterns you employ. These characteristics establish the relationship between structural elements that in itself can guide a reader or audience; but they also contain information in themselves, the patterns suggesting ways you envisage the things being shown or told.

Conventions of Structure

Form and genre provide two of the most prominent framing devices for considering structural convention. Formal poetry and screenplays are obvious examples with reasonably well-known structural conventions and, to an extent, expectations. But there are many conventions of size and shape that provide us, as writers, with guidelines to what are recognizable structural characteristics of completed works of creative writing. In his doctoral dissertation, completed at the University of Exeter in 2012, Richard Heeks provides a succinct outline of the mediating aspect of genre. He writes:

> Genre, however, is a complex form of mediation, in that genre categories both reflect and construct how a text is understood. Subcategories of short stories, for example, such as fairy tales, the modern short story, or Dirty Realism (a form of 1980s short story realism), each provides different frameworks for how texts are understood and interpreted. Genre offers a pattern and key for the understanding of texts, in this way, that is valuable and sympathetic at the same time as being somewhat controlling. (Heeks, 2012: 22)

Recognition of structural conventions is not limited to writers; there is a shared cultural recognition of creative writing structures. Most non-writers recognize a poem, a play or a short story. They recognize the form and, when experiencing the work, they often fairly quickly pick up the genre. Of course, instances of writers subverting convention are far from rare. Such subversion is both a creative enterprise and a challenge to popular perception of a writing structure.

Needless to say, structural convention and the subverting of structural convention tend toward suggesting a work is mainstream or it is experimental. Nothing unusual in that, given that what we call 'experimental' generally is what confronts expectation. Interestingly, though, writing genre tends to be based on recognizable content or style. So to subvert structural convention in genre doubly challenges expectation. For this reason, it is more often we hear about 'cross-genre' or 'multi-genre' works – suggesting that conventions (structural and otherwise) remain but are joined together or amalgamated for the overall effect.

Metaphors for Structure

Architecture, perhaps most obviously, offers a comprehensive and potentially productive metaphor for investigating and understanding structure in creative writing. Architecture refers to design, in its literal sense design by people, though we sometimes see 'architecture' used figuratively to refer to natural designs or even to things that are not so much designed as found in the world. Interestingly, often the idea of architecture attaches itself to parts of the built environment that are seen to have aesthetic value, that are considered to be beautiful, that transcend the ordinary, go beyond functionality. The art of architecture is thus attached to the science of architecture, the ingenuity and imaginativeness of construction to the engineering fundamentals of construction – and in this metaphoric sense is ideal to refer to creative writing. As linguist Karen Sullivan (2013: 3) points out, 'metaphoric language depends not only on the choice of words, but also on particular grammatical constructions'.

Some other metaphoric structural guides relating to creative writing could also be seen as literal guides – the notion of a journey for example, in which structure is related to geography and the mapping of a route from start to finish of that journey. The idea of movement here is, of course, significant, in that creative writing is based on action, empowered by movement from one idea, one scene, one image, one character, one event to another. Journeys are core to much creative writing – whether these are physical journeys or journeys of the mind. But the notion of a journey can also provide a structural metaphor in that there is a beginning point, stops along the way, an ending (or we could say 'destination'). That ending can signify reaching the point at which you are satisfied as a writer and you believe (predict, more accurately, perhaps) that your audience will be satisfied. Again, in metaphoric terms, the sense of having reached a destination to which you were heading, the anticipation as you head toward that destination, the new sights seen or people encountered, the ending bringing full meaning to the journey.

Mathematical metaphors, likewise, are also potentially literal guides. So, you imagine your poem or your novel like a mathematical formula in which the structure is based on the ideas of addition, subtraction, multiplication or division. Sections, lines,

internal patterns of sentences, all potentially part of the metaphoric equation. 'You write it all', says Annie Dillard,

> Discovering it at the end of a line of words. The line of words is
> a fiber optic, flexible as wire; it illuminates the path just before
> its fragile tip. (Dillard, 1989: 7)

The figurative context here is that by doing this you are
attempting, in colloquial terms, to come to some decision about
'what adds up' structurally. This equation – like any mathematical puzzle – is aiming to solve the problem you are posing. For
example, you wish to tell the story of an event, involving a number of smaller events, some people, historical context, alternative
ways of viewing the main event. The mathematical metaphor
here might be one of intersecting lines, vectors, coefficients,
coordinates, geometry, fractions, symmetry and so on. That
metaphor could guide how you weight the number of words
spent on parts of the work, and how you use resonance and in
what ways you determine viewpoint. Alternatively, math can, of
course, be a literal guide – so the poet who is writing a sonnet
and knows the traditional count of 14 lines, or the novelist who
uses a general sense of number of chapters and size of chapters to
assist them in constructing their work, or the screenwriter who
maps number of pages onto projected screen time, aiming for a
mainstream cinematic release of their film where film length can
be one element defining the strength of audience interest.

Structural metaphors help emphasize that while structure
is a physical property, it is also a property of how we organize our thoughts and how we, in some ways, make sense of
the creations of our imaginations. When we think figuratively
about structure, we aim to empower our sense-making, taking what can be viewed as formally imposed mechanics and
enlivening the surface of construction with the underpinning of
inventiveness.

Structures and Meaning

As much described here suggests, structures are not merely
containers for topics, ideas, images and stories. Structures provide an embodiment of what might otherwise be transcendental,

what is incorporeal – our emotions, our thoughts. Structures contain meaning and structures also promote types of meaning – literal, comparative, cultural, linguistic, personal, gendered and so on. Keeping the architectural metaphor in mind, Robert Hershberger, writing in *The Journal of Aesthetic Education*, offers this on architecture and meaning:

> it is held that if there is a primary purpose for architecture, it is not communication or meaning at all, but provision. The central purpose of architecture is to provide shelter, protection, and accommodation for the physical activities of man. The communication function of architecture is necessary, however, to guide people into using buildings as intended and to enrich the experience of so doing. Meaning is, therefore, a necessary part of what makes a building architecture, but it is not sufficient. It is important that a building communicate its ability to shelter, protect, and accommodate; but it is equally or more important that it does in fact shelter, protect, and accommodate. (Hershberger, 1970: 39)

The relationship noted by Hershberger between 'provision' and 'meaning', and what this might entail in terms of structure, carries relevance also for us as writers. His reference to communicating is, of course, basic in our own practice and in our works, given that the central purpose of all writing is communication. However, because creative writing uses the imagination to consider everything from the firmly factual and the counterfactual but possible, to the wildly fantastical, the range of communicative meaning is considerable. Unlike those arts not using as commonplace a tool as written language (music, for example, with its often uncommon sounds and compositional forms, its specific instruments, particular venues), creative writing makes the very common exceptional by communicating meaning in layered and interrelational ways. Such communication impacts on the structures we use in creative writing. For example, while a chapter in a novel might appear at first glance much like a chapter in an instruction manual or like a chapter in an academic monograph, the heightened use of such things as resonance, metaphor and allusion makes it distinctive. As does, perhaps, changes of viewpoint, perhaps graphic alterations of sectioning points, perhaps dialogue, patterns of description and exposition that go beyond a simple informational format.

Meaning, also, is contextual – how something is said, to whom, where and when. Thus, our structures too need to be viewed contextually. What a structural characteristic means to one reader will therefore be the product of history and culture, education, experience and personal psychology. Certainly, some of these meanings will be shared – thus the reference to culture – but some will be highly localized to a person, a place, a time. Such situational meaning, when it relates to structure, explains why literature from earlier periods of human history is sometimes not only considered anachronistic because of language or tone but also because of how things are arranged within it, its form and the organization of its elements.

Ultimately, meaning is a relationship. It involves our mental processes and our behaviors. Structures in creative writing therefore attempt to convey to a reader or audience the results of the mental processes the writer has applied, the behaviors we are attempting to convey, the meaning you, as the writer, find in these. Such attempts at shared meaning are aided by structure, given that in creative writing so much can be located beyond simple communicative statements and that structure can work as signposts and signals of meaning that can be complex and multifarious.

Acts of Structuring

Our acts of structuring are clearly organizing acts, part of the movement and flow of our writing, generally. Active structuring suggests the existence of a process. That is, when structuring you are orchestrating, arranging things, sometimes bringing together disparate elements (for example, the visual and the historical or the personal and the public) or placing elements in a specific order or relationship with one another. All in the interests of producing something that carries meaning – the meaning you intend.

Using the writing tools available to you – whether these tools are those of grammar and punctuation, word selection and combination, appearance, pace, juxtaposition and contrast – you are effectively attempting to relate subject and theme to arrangement and orchestration. This is universally true, but is not always as obvious in some writing forms as others. For example, formal poetry and the screenplay are highly structured and these structures are highly visible and widely used. Short stories less so, comparatively at least, free verse, of course – structures are there, but less obviously so. Structuring does not mean to limit, though it can mean to choose. In 1958, well-known Shakespearean scholar Aerol Arnold wrote in the journal *American Quarterly*:

> The area of experience which the author chooses to write about is the raw material: it is what he starts with; it is what he must reflect upon, select from, distort or impose a shape upon, so that it will mean to the reader what he, the author, feels that it means. As I use the term 'structure' it is everything that is done to explore the significance of the raw material - the experience of life - and to shape it so that the reader's response to it is directed and, to some extent, controlled. (Arnold, 1958: 327)

'Everything that is *done*' Arnold reflects, seeing structure not as something that independently exists but as something that is always shaped and produced by a writer. Structure, therefore, is an empowering element, both for writer and for reader or audience – because it provides context, knowledge, direction and a point of association, exchanged between the maker and the receiver.

Speaking of structure from the two writerly points of view – (1) structuring as specific actions of writing and (2) structuring as a textual activity, whereby a final work emerges and can be said to be 'structured', to have a 'structure' – the methods you employ to consider structure and the ways in which structuring can be used, and can be empowering of your meaning and of your intentions, are considerable.

Beginning with structural metaphors, how structures mean offers opportunities to underpin what meanings image, story, viewpoint and tone in your work also support. Structure has cultural and symbolic messaging – the structure of a motor vehicle, a revolving door, a chair, a ladder, by and large indicates their use. Within reason, that is – if you are from a similar culture, similar time. The same goes for structures in creative writing: structure sends a message.

This messaging provided by structure informs a response from a reader, contributing to their understanding. Occasionally, a writer might subvert this fact. Much like the cardboard box that becomes a child's cave, a bedroom that becomes a study or a sword that becomes a living room decor, a structure can be re-purposed. In doing so, a writer might aim to unsettle or draw attention to artifice or even to question traditions of structure themselves. We have seen this graphically in the use of footnotes and annotations in works such as Flann O'Brien's *The Third Policeman* (1967), Mark E. Danielewski's *House of Leaves* (2000) and Vladimir Nabokov's *Pale Fire* (1962).

Structure, referring to the arrangement of things, to a shape, a design, a layout, offers you the opportunity to consider the nature of shaping, designing and laying out in different creative writing genre, in different periods of literary history and in different cultures. You can draw from this information to help in determining what contemporary notions exist, and how they impact on both the actions of writers and the expectations of readers. You can also use this information to increase the range of shaping choices – perhaps some of which existed in history, or exist in other cultures, but have not been widely used of late. Structure seen as laying out similarly affords you opportunities to imagine your work as a kind of topographical map over which you have control – arranging the positioning of each element, whether it is visible on the high ground (so to speak) or layered lower in the profile of the work. You might even use such a figurative notion to consider where key topographical features – metaphorically speaking the cities, the mountains, the distinctive features – of your work are going to lie.

Finally, structure is the constitution of a work. It is an indicator of fundamental principles and of what you imagine as the fabric of what you are making and what you are presenting. In a very similar way, the structure of your writing life, your writing environment, is an indicator of fundamental principles. This can be explored further through a wider consideration of process. But, in every element and in every case, it is in using and considering structure we also declare our ability to choose. Robert Pinsky, poet, translator and critic, who served as Poet Laureate Consultant in Poetry to the Library of Congress from 1997 to 2000, refers to this when he discusses poetic form in his book *Poetry and the World*:

> A poem may be the least confused, most free thing one says (or hears) because it is the most deliberately physical, and so the most naked. Form expresses the craving to be free of imposed, controlling abstractions. It is a made, bodily abstraction to challenge the abstractions of circumstances. (Pinsky, 1988: 169)

References

Arnold, A. (1958) Why structure in fiction: A note to social scientists. *American Quarterly* 10 (3), 325–337.

Dillard, A. (1989) *The Writing Life*. New York: Harper and Row.

Heeks, R. (2012) Discovery Writing and Genre. ProQuest Dissertations Publishing. See https://ore.exeter.ac.uk/repository/handle/10871/13802 (accessed 18 August 2019).

Hershberger, R.G. (1970) Architecture and meaning. *Journal of Aesthetic Education* 4 (4), 37–55.

Morgan, B. and Perez, M. (2013) *On Story: Screenwriters and Their Craft*. Austin, TX: University of Texas.

Pinsky, R. (1988) *Poetry and the World*. Hopewell, NJ: Ecco.

Sartre, J.-P. (1971) *Words*. Harmondsworth: Penguin.

Stevick, P. (1970) *The Chapter in Fiction: Theories of Narrative Division*. Syracuse, NY: Syracuse University Press.

Sullivan, K. (2013) *Frames and Constructions in Metaphoric Language*. Amsterdam: John Benjamins.

Thomas, D.M. (1988) *Memories and Hallucinations: A Memoir*. New York: Penguin.

3 Movement, Flow, Process

Because writing is essentially words on a page (literally written there, or figuratively 'inscribed' on a screen), its ability to convey motion is entirely dependent on suggestion, on its indications of movement. As an art, creative writing appears therefore to be unlike film or the theater, to be unlike making music. Creative writing, in appearance, seems essentially static.

Of course, in many other ways, we know this not to be true. Creative writing is powered by and dependent on motion because motion is essential for human communication – some kind of exchange between people being what we mean by communication, including the control and application of a rhythm, rises and falls in tone and in pitch, graphic notations that vary so that the reader's eye is encouraged to move, across and down and along... all of this is motion or suggesting motion.

Movement and flow as they relate to your actions as a creative writer, your compositional practices, how you undertake these, how you order these, how you relate these to each other. Movement relates to your ways of gathering material, patterns of drafting, how you physically inscribe things (with a pencil, by typing on a keyboard, even the physicality of reading into a recording device), the flow of your time and the physical interaction through the space you inhabit. *Movement* relates to potentially disjointed or disparate gestures, disconnected or abrupt changes or fluctuations – so, when you stop writing one thing and begin writing another, or when your compositional practices involve your seeking out information rather than inscribing words on a page, or when someone interrupts you writing and you abandon it for the day. *Flow*, alternatively, references a steady, continuous activity, where a writing project is begun and ultimately continues (sometimes in a steady fashion) until it is completed. Creative writing can involve both these, many types and instances of movement and the presence of a progressive 'flow' toward a project's completion. Joyce Carol Oates chooses words that reflect upon her concept of writing flow:

> Writing, for me, is primarily remembering. Which means that writing' isn't specifically verbal for me, as it must be for most poets: it's as likely to be cinematic, dramatic, emotional, auditory, and shimmeringly unformed before it becomes actual language, transformed into words on a page.... I spend much of my time away from the study, in fact. I spend much of my time in motion. Running (my favorite activity, in which my metabolism seems somehow 'normal'), walking, bicycling. Driving a car (cruise control recommended) or being driven in one. In airports, on airplanes. So often, airports and airplanes! (Oates, 2004: 141)

Movement and flow here also, of course, relate to the object that is produced – because works of creative writing are ultimately physical objects. These objects are, plainly, an art and a type of communication offered in words (so, not primarily images or sounds, for example). Here then, how your writing is offered, what patterns of words you have created, how you present that pattern. How that pattern you have created has a surface (say, the appearance of a line of poetry or a sentence of a short story or the uses of punctuation to suggest pauses or the frequency of verbs used), and has an undercurrent as in, say, the connotations, the resonances created with previous ideas or observations in the work, through synonymously referring to them; or the reference to external events that themselves have a well-known sequence of happenings.

Movement, in that a work of creative writing can have a range of 'gestures' (using gestures here to refer to expressions and signals). These guide the reader or audience to the meaning of a passage or a section, a moment in a scene or an entire work's collection of intentions and outlooks, things you wish to show and tell, ways of understanding you wish to suggest. Flow, in that a work of creative writing has an overarching aesthetic, even if its internal patterns are varied (in fact, perhaps because its internal patterns are varied!). Flow as the definition of how a work in its entirety presents itself to those who receive it. Flow as the passage through the work, its heading toward a final point, a conclusion – which might in the sense of flow not be final at all, because a work of creative writing can linger with its reader, create memories that continue on, not so much end as send its audience onward.

And *process*. Process relates to both movement and flow. However, process suggests a more structured enterprise, a conscious address to both movement and flow. Process involves steps, and a series of actions. Process also tends to be expressly focused on a particular outcome. In a book edited by Daniel Halpern, entitled *Who's Writing This?*, in which writers create versions of themselves and tell their story, prolific American writer John Updike writes about ('his') steps to begin writing:

> I brush my teeth, I dress and descend to the kitchen, where I eat and read the newspaper, which has been dreaming its own dreams all night. Postponing the moment, savoring every small news item and vitamin pill and sip of unconcentrated orange juice, I at last return to the upstairs and face the rooms that Updike has filled with his books, his papers, his trophies, his projects. The abundant clutter stifles me, yet I am helpless to clear away much of it. It would be blasphemy. He has become a sacred reality to me. I gaze at his worn wooden desk, his boxes of dull pencils, his blank-faced word processor, with religious fear.
>
> Suppose some day, he fails to show up? I would attempt to do his work, but no one would be fooled. (Halpern, 1985: 183)

If a creative writer has a process – and we can explore general processes that occur for a writer across all or many projects, or a singular process related to the writing of a single work – then that process will be an orchestration of actions, so that you might (for example) have such things in mind as:

• *How long do you typically spend on a project?* If you begin writing a novel, would you expect to finish it in, say, 10 weeks or in 10 years? The Electric Literature website offers an infographic that explains that Audrey Niffenegger took four years to write *The Time Traveler's Wife*, while William Faulkner wrote *As I Lay Dying* in six weeks. *Nineteen Eighty-Four* took

George Orwell a year to write, while Robert Louis Stevenson wrote *The Strange Case of Dr. Jekyll and Mr. Hyde* in six days (Electric Literature). Virginia Woolf, in a diary entry of Tuesday, November 23, 1926, considering her pace of writing (or, more accurately, lack of pace) declares:

> I am re-doing six pages of Lighthouse daily. This is not so quick as Mrs D.: but then I find much of it sketchy, & have to improvise on the typewriter. (Bell, 1982: 117)

Those perhaps informal rules of thumb relate to process – in this case, length of time taken and how your time is then applied. This directly relates to why you write (for example, for personal satisfaction, mostly, or do you also write for commercial purposes?) and where creative writing fits in your life (for example, do you write between doing another job, or do you write full-time?).

• *In what order will you draft your project?* Some writers might collect all the material they need to inform their writing of a project (as lightly done as some scribbled thoughts or as heavily supported as years of evidence). Others might set out on a project with only the barest of thought or simply an inspired sense, discovering where the project is going and what it entails as they progress. As a writer, you might typically start with a key scene or a line, or some descriptions or plot out a set of characters, and then weave the rest of the project around this. More typically, you might simply start at the beginning and, at some point, sense you have an ending in sight. Are there typical indications to you of where that beginning might be, and do you generally know when a project is ending? That's an indication of a process.

• *Drafting and revision: how much and when?* There is simply no fixed amount of drafting that ultimately produces a completed work of creative writing. However, there are cultural assumptions – about literature, about art, about human effort versus human results – that completed written works of importance involve a great deal of honing. Perhaps so! But not always. And we also have to consider how much writing work occurs before we define ourselves as actually 'writing' (widespread actions and influences such as thinking, questioning, experiencing, for example). There is also the question of when we're drafting and when we're revising – taking 'drafting' to refer to initiating and building up a base of material and 'revising' to refer to making it more like what we want, more sharply the piece we seek to create, to get it closer to how we might like it when it's complete. There might not be a fixed amount to any of this, but as part of your writing process you develop a sense of where drafting ends and revising begins, and in this creation of compositional process you institute actions that reflect what place in the sequence your current project appears to be. Mario Vargas Llosa notes:

> The process of writing is something in which a writer's whole personality plays a part. A writer writes not only with his ideas but also with his instincts, his intuition. (Llosa, 1991: 39)

• *Is your typical plan to keep a work entirely to yourself until it is done, or do you show earlier versions to other people?* Your process might be action orientated – you have a way of behaving that is largely internalized and confirmed by you – or it can be *inter*active – you have a way of behaving that involves the input of others. Which others, when and why? If your process is only to reveal a completed work when you confirm for yourself that it is completed, how do you reveal it – in print through a publisher, in manuscript, online, in a live reading?

These are simply some examples of what we might refer to as 'creative writing process'. Process gives structure to movement and flow. We can generally discover a great deal about creative writing by analyzing elements of movement and flow in how we work, and in our works, as well as in the working and works of others. The reason this is true is because words inscribed on a page (or figuratively on a screen) are essentially static, but language and communication are animated. How we create with words, empower ideas and emotions in words, empower our imagination and the imagination of others, has a lot to do with the actions we take and the dynamism in the works we produce.

We generally recognize a difference between movement and stasis, between activity and inactivity, between flow and standstill. The science of motion is complex, but some of its basic laws (for example, those associated with mathematician and physicist, Isaac Newton, 1643–1727) are known to us colloquially. The ideas associated with these laws broadly inform our ways of acting and reacting in the world. Newton's third law, 'for every action, there is an equal and opposite reaction', finds its way not only into mechanics but also into moral codes and social interactions. Similarly, while Newton's first and second laws – 'every object persists in its state of rest or uniform motion in a straight line unless there is force applied to it' and 'force equals mass times acceleration' – might not be topics of casual conversation, they are familiar to many of us in some way. Simply try to deflect a thrown ball or apply pressure to open a can of tuna and you are applying your casual sense of these laws.

Understanding movement and flow is as important to us as it is not only because we seek to get around but also because we exist in a life narrative that is understood through movement. The movement from birth to death, for example – which carries with it a sense of us as developing creatures, who begin life with limited understanding and become more informed, who start out small and grow to full size. There are movements associated with seasons or with the transitions from day to night, and the flow that is associated with waking or sleeping, continuousness being the contingent aspect defining us as being 'awake' or 'sleeping well'. There are the processes we encounter that order activities in our world (whether it is the steps taken in education, from first formal encounter to final graduation; or the order in an annual tax return system, the filing, the assessing, the result of the assessment; or the procedures in medical practice, most often followed due to previous positive results, and associated with being a medical professional; or the ways we build our homes, our schools, our office blocks; or the steps we take to enact laws and governmental policies, or the cyclical and intentional aspects of growing crops for food or the operational contingencies of managing motor vehicle traffic…).

Movement, flow and process clearly exist in our world, they are part of how we think and they influence how we feel. As we creative writers are working with the written language, creating with it and producing final objects that are largely (most often entirely) made up of our written languages, we can benefit from understanding the movement, flow and process in our actions. We can benefit also from considering how our completed works represent, produce a sense of and utilize such tools in our communication with other people.

Imagine how anyone could begin to inscribe a poem without movement, or complete a screenplay without flow. Similarly imagine how a work of creative writing would look, reach its audience or produce any communication, how it would spark our curiosity or emotional reaction or encourage contemplation if it showed no change of any kind. Here, screenwriter Nicholas Kazan considers such change in terms of character:

> There is a point at which, if he just simply stops and decides whatever it is he wanted in the picture is not worth it, he can always get back to life he led before. So I look for that moment when something happens, and mostly I want it to happen because the character – it grows out of the character's qualities and the nature of the man or the woman – does something that pushes him past the point of no return. From that point on, he can never get his old life back. He has to go forward into unknown territory. (Morgan & Perez, 2013: 73)

Creative Writing Actions

Actions can be spontaneous, fleeting and unplanned, or deliberate, enduring and well planned. We sometimes find in the teaching of the arts, whether the writing arts or the theater arts, whether filmmaking or music making, that there is institutional encouragement to favor the latter, and in this way produce an ordered, logical creative writing curriculum. In other words, that because (perhaps!) of the nature of contemporary mainstream education, we are encouraged to formalize how we might deliver the aims and objectives of the teaching we offer, and ultimately the outcomes for learners. This we can call 'the romance of process', in which we suggest a more structured series of steps with a particular (in this case readily identifiable and assessable) result in mind.

The actions in your creative writing can certainly involve process. That is, what you do can be structured and the actions you undertake can occur in a deliberate series. So, for example, you might write at certain times of the day or week and revise or edit your work at other times, and you might compose in to and fro movement until a draft is complete or alternatively compose in a linear way until a draft is done, and then return to the beginning. Your process might be your salvation, giving you confidence to continue and complete a work. It might be your guide, providing you with information about where you are in your composing and what you should do next. Nevertheless, some writers fear even a discussion of process, sensing something beyond set actions is at play. In that vein, young adult fiction writer Katherine Paterson says this:

> An author who speaks about his own books is almost as bad as a mother who talks about her own children. I'm not sure what Disraeli would have to say about a person who was guilty on both counts. But the real danger in talking about your work is not simply that you'll prove boring to your listener, though you probably will, but that you'll do damage to the imaginative process. (Bridgers *et al.*, 1987: 17)

Admittedly, Paterson appears to be using the word process more generically here to mean ways of writing. Certainly, creative writing, with its imaginative leaps and inventiveness, can't only be based on a set process (though whether talking about a process is a dangerous thing is entirely up for debate!). Too rigid a sense of the steps involved and their series would do little to empower creativity, employ inspiration or explore relationships between ideas and feelings. Instead of the romance of process, the reality of creative writing is more in the realm of interactions and interrelations – in essence, some actions we can describe as movement, some as components of a flow and some as part of our process.

• *Movement?* Discovering what movements occur in your creative writing is preparation for understanding why they occur. Imagine that you determine that the viewpoint of your story is entirely wrong. So wrong that you abandon the draft you have been working on and start writing the story again. Such change can be disconcerting if you have a sense of writing being largely a linear, forward-moving enterprise. The stories of writers who have given up on a project, or on creative writing altogether, because 'it wasn't working' would fill a substantial volume. But if we consider change, shifts of direction and reconsiderations as natural elements of the creatively and critically aware movement in our writing, then we produce more productive and ultimately useable reactions to change. In this case, what made you consider that the viewpoint was not working? Why was it so 'wrong' that you had to begin again?

Other movements might be less a case of direction changing, but part of a random pattern of associations and actions that drive your imagination and stimulate your intellect. So, for example, something happens in your day, some observation during a social encounter, or a piece of news or a natural event (a storm, a change in the color of the light) and you find yourself incorporating something of any of those things into the work or works you're composing. You could not describe that compositional action as part of a continuity or part of a process; and yet, it is certainly relevant, and it is certainly influential. Interaction and interrelation, these are the clues to discovering (and applying) knowledge about how you write creatively.

• *Flow?* Simply taking the meaning here as 'continuing', all creative writing has to involve flow. How steady that flow is, how long maintained and how continuous can be the result of many factors from the time available to you to write, to the commitment you have to write in the first place, to whether you have the technical skills to overcome difficulties in your composing, to how you feel, psychologically, about continuity. Some people prefer alternating activities, concentrate better in small or medium bursts and dislike the perceived monotony in sustained, consistent action. Discovering what continuing creative writing means for you could be a case of determining (a) what you consider to be progress when you are writing and (b) how you imagine an outcome of the writing that you are doing. For example, is the end result the only outcome, or the experience of writing or the satisfaction in expressing yourself creatively – any of these, other things?

• *Process?* If you can determine the structure of your creative writing actions, determine a series of actions, then it is logically more likely that you can repeat that series. Or challenge one or more of those steps in it, of course, because it could be that the process you discover is flawed. Poet Philip Larkin considered that 'self-consciousness' could damage his skill and 'poetic theory' not be 'much good if it hinders the poet'; nevertheless, he frequently considered ideas and influences on how and what he wrote:

> what one writes depends so much on one's character and environment – either one writes about them or to escape from them – it follows that, basically, no one more chooses what one writes than one chooses the character one has or the environment one has. (Larkin, 2001: 79)

Analyzing the steps you take, the series of those steps and the actions they incorporate, you could surmise the weakness is specific to the project at hand or it is something about how you approach writing generally that needs to be done differently. Steps might need reordering or additional steps added. You might find it is not the process that is flawed – considering the steps taken, their extent and their ordering is fine – but that the idea you have hasn't got enough depth to sustain the work, that it is the content not the structure of your actions that needs reconsidering. Of course, you might also discover you have a process, it is all you would want it to be, and its impact on the results of your writing is exactly as you'd desire, and you are entirely satisfied!

Types of creative writing motion to investigate here include:

Compositional choice making – you can consider what factors influence your decision-making when writing, and how these choices relate to how you act. The motion of your writing reflects and is reflected in compositional choices – for example, choose to use dialogue rather than narration and the forward movement of a short story is paused or slows down.

Sequential acts – when completing one element in your writing, is another plainly suggested to you? So, you act on some preconceived notions of progress. This sense of things could be considered the core to your process.

Fortuitousness – the impact of the unexpected, and how this alters or reaffirms the pace of your writing, the direction, the inclusions, your sense of what comes next in the work.

Inter-textual influences – both your previous works and the works of others can play a role in determining a sense of what actions are needed. For example, you know many of your previous short stories are constructed in short, named sections. You either follow that pattern again, working in a way that sees each section complete, or you deem to use an alternate structure. Textual assessments in this way influence your future text making.

Environmental factors – when you feel it is too hot or too cold, your pace of writing might be interrupted. When it is quiet, or when you're overlooking the streets your writing about, or when you encounter family or friends.... The way you write, how fast you write, how often you write, all are influenced by environment.

Access to techniques – limitations on your technical prowess can influence how you write – not least in the time taken to complete a particular task, or whether you undertake it at all. What writing techniques you can and do employ produce a rhythm of composition.

Outside influences – the role of other people, from the basics of interrupting your writing progress or encouraging your progress, to the complexities of interpersonal relations, editorial advice and, in some cases, the demands of contractual deadlines. In some ways, you might not always have control over the movement, flow and process in your creative writing – how you would wish to do things could well be influenced by how you *have* to do things.

Works of Creative Writing

Works of creative writing also reveal and present motion – that is, movement, flow and process. In general, they need to represent these states because human communication references types of motion, language involving exchange of meaning, understanding the written word being dependent on its representation of actions, things and people that are not literally the words themselves but to what the words refer. Such signification itself involves movement – from the signifier (the word) to the signified (that to which it refers). Writing, quite simply, involves the motion between the static inscriptions on a page or screen and the things, meanings, experiences and so forth, to which those words refer.

When talking about works of creative writing, motion is often discussed in terms of rhythm or of pace, and often these are discussed in relation to patterns displayed in the text. However, much textual analysis assumes (and begins) at the presence of the text, the finished work or occasionally the finished work and the textual evidence of its making (earlier drafts, writing evidence such as planning notes). Alternatively, if we as writers consider works of creative writing from the point of view of creating them, then we are talking about motion in terms of writing tools used, and in relation to writing choices. Of course, the pace, the motion needed for creating a work might not match the pace, the motion depicted in a work. Jan Baetens and Kathryn Hume reference something of this in their discussion in the journal *Narrative*:

> The impossibility of writing as fast as one can think is a common complaint in confessions and testimonies by authors on their own practice. The most famous is perhaps that made by Blaise Pascal: '*En écrivant ma pensée elle m'échappe quelquefois ; mais cela me fait souvenir de ma faiblesse que j'oublie à toute heure, ce qui m'instruit autant que ma pensée oubliée, car je ne tiens qu'à connaître mon néant*' (Pascal 1115) [In writing down my thought, it sometimes escapes me; but this makes me remember my weakness, that I constantly forget. This is as instructive to me as my forgotten thought; for I strive only to know my nothingness. (Trotter)] (Baetens & Hume, 2006: 350)

• *Movement*. In a work of creative writing, movement and meaning are closely related. If we think of movement as gestures (that is, as expressions and signals), then movement in (say) a novel or a poem is used to introduce, strengthen or alter meaning. If expressions guide the reader, they also set the tone of the work and they suggest the relationship between the work and its audience. So expressions – that is, how things are made known – can create closeness or distance between the work and its audience. They can establish and order a relationship between what's being said and to whom it is being said. Gestures, as signals, alert the reader to when they should pay particular attention and to what. They display an attitude. So, the movement in a work of creative writing is brought about by how things are made known and in what ways and how this guides the reader or audience.

• *Flow.* A work of creative writing will also have a flow – in this case referring to continuousness. This is the overall patterning of the work, the movements within it arranged as a concerted whole. Although there might be variation, changes in tempo, points of focus that slow the work and summary material that moves it apace, graphic signals of where a reader might momentarily pause, changes in word choice and association that alter the pulse of the work, there will nevertheless be an overarching aesthetic that creates the flow.

• *Process.* It might seem strange to suggest that a work of creative writing can have a process. While we can identify 'movement' in a text, and even suggest a text has a defining 'flow', the idea that a work of creative writing can display a process seems less certain. After all, process refers to a series of *actions* undertaken, while a text is a material thing. However, imagine we are talking about communication and in this case a process of creative communication between writer and reader or audience, a structured engagement in making and receiving this communication. Alexander Spektor alludes to this exchange in his work on Russian poet and essayist Osip Emilyevich Mandelstam, and Mandlestam's reading of the poet, Dante:

> Therefore, the main drive of Mandel'shtam's writings on the naturalists is to conceptualize what can be described as a *physiology of writing*, from which there is but half a step to what he terms the physiology of reading: "The *physiology of reading* still remains to be studied.... "Mandel'shtam does this by interpreting the naturalists' scientific discourse as artistic discourse but also by adapting their methods of interpreting and classifying the organic world to his analysis

of their own writings. This allows for the possibility of what Mandel'shtam calls "organic thinking," necessary in order for us to "come close to the mysteries of organic life." Vision and instinct are required if one seeks to penetrate the mysteries of life; the possession of both unites the naturalists with Dante. Just like the naturalists, who are able to understand the hidden processes governing organic life, Dante's comparisons penetrate the surface: they are not descriptive, argues Mandel'shtam, but "always pursue the concrete task of presenting the inner form of the poem's structure or driving force. (Spektor, 2014: 481)

Process in the text then refers to the series of operations that make that communication successful (or not successful). Process in a work of creative writing in this sense is a combination of your text's appearance, the ideas it presents and explores, the relationship between its genre and the literary conventions of that genre, its internal effects (viewpoint, tone, point of view and so forth), all of which contribute to the process of communication.

Exploring movement, flow and process does not mean defaulting to everything becoming process – in the sense being suggested here that process refers to the conscious, the structured, the calculated, the sequential. That is, an investigation of your creative writing, perhaps also through your creative writing, does not mean your critical analysis shuts down all options for the unexpected, the fortuitous, the new and the original. Your imagination has the ability to deal with the factual, the counterfactual and the fantastic. It can inform a procedural approach where you choose to do things at certain times and in certain places, and where those things are planned and conscious. But your imagination is also able to enlighten your actions related to the unexpected, the impromptu and the random. To dismiss the existence of such things would be to deny creativity many of its attributes. Your creative writing – both how you do it and what you produce when you do it – will contain movement, flow *and* process. Each contributes to how you view your writing successes and your writing goals.

References

Baetens, J. and Hume, K. (2006) Speed, rhythm, movement: A dialogue on K. Hume's article 'Narrative Speed'. *Narrative* 14 (3), 349–355.

Bell, A.O. (ed.) (1982) *The Diary of Virginia Woolf: Volume III: 1925–30.* Harmondsworth: Penguin.

Bridgers, S.E., Lipsyte, R., Meltzer, M. and Paterson, K. (1987) Facets: YA authors talk about their writing. *The English Journal* 76 (3), 14–17.

Electric Literature. See https://electricliterature.com/infographic-how-long-did-famous-novels-take-to-write/ (accessed 11 August 2019).

Halpern, D. (1985) *Who's Writing This?* Hopewell, NJ: Ecco.

Larkin, P. (2001) *Further Requirements: Interviews, Broadcasts, Statements and Book Reviews, 1952–1985.* London: Faber.

Llosa, M.V. (1991) *A Writer's Reality.* London: Faber.

Morgan, B. and Perez, M. (2013) *On Story: Screenwriters and Their Craft.* Austin, TX: University of Texas.

Oates, J.C. (2004) *The Faith of a Writer: Life, Craft, Art.* New York: Ecco.

Spektor, A. (2014) The science of poetry: Poetic process as evolution in Mandel'shtam's 'Conversation about Dante'. *Slavic Review* 73 (3), 471–493.

4 Knowing Your Influences

Few of us live in complete isolation from everything and everyone. Rather, we experience (and reflect in our writing) the influences of our cultures, the geographic area in which we live, the things we do beyond creative writing, hobbies, sports, other jobs, the local or national or international events that happen all around us now, or that happened in the past, the influences of things we read or that we watch. Our writing is also influenced by our closest associations – our family, friends, colleagues. It is obviously influenced too by our own personalities, our individual psychologies. Cliché as it might sound, influences on our creative writing are indeed everywhere and come in a great many forms. This fact on its own does little to assist us in improving our creative writing. Rather, it is our ability to understand the influences that can empower us to better engage with, and leverage, those influences. We can in this more productively assess them and consider them in relation to what we want to achieve in our creative writing. Novelist, short-story writer and philosopher William Gass is speaking of influence and influencing when he remarks:

> Culture not only contains our written and spoken languages, it is itself a larger language: a set of rules and directives, orders and ordinances, which enable our actions to become significant, which bind us together in the same system of signs. (Gass, 1986: 191)

Influences also have specificity – that is, we can identify them – and they have magnitude – that is, we can consider the strength of them. Influences can be long term or short term. So, it might be that we write frequently about our local region as did the American writer William Faulkner or that we explore particular themes by focusing on a particular culture and periods of history, as does Nigerian writer Chinua Achebe, whose works draw on traditional Igbo society and consider the clash of values brought about by imperialism. It might be that who we imagine to be our audience is connected to those we spend most time with in our social life or our work life. It might be that we are influenced mostly by our entertainment activities, our reading, watching or game-playing lives – activities that take us beyond the real world into somewhere other, even somewhere fantastical. It might be that when we write and how we write are influenced by how much time we have to write, and that, in that basic yet significant way, we choose writing techniques and genre and writing aims that can best be managed given the time we have at our disposal.

Exploring creative writing influences, and discovering what they are, how they might impact on us, how regularly and how intensively they might impact on us and in what ways we might use some of them gives us not only an understanding of what influences us, but also leverage with those influences that are in our control.

We can differentiate influences on our creative writing based on some being 'internal' and some being 'external'. Internal, in this sense, including those things that are emotional or influential because they are part of our personalities or that are the result of our education, what we believe we know or that relate to our sense of identity, our sense of self. External including those things that are happening around us while we are writing, the local or even global events that attract our attention, or that impact because they are aspects of the world generally, past or present, and that we draw upon in our writing – in terms of subject or theme, perhaps. Clearly, considering this, there is not a complete separation of internal and external influences on us. Our emotions, our intellectual interests, our sensibilities, while informed by our personalities, by our 'nature', are certainly impacted upon by 'nurture', the experiences we have and the things happening around us. African-American poet, writer and dramatist Mari Evans says this:

Who I am is central to how I write and what I write; and I am the continuation of my father's passage. I have written for as long as I have been aware of writing as a way of setting down feelings and the stuff of imaginings. (Evans, 1985: 167)

Determining the range and extent of influences on our creative writing is therefore not simply a case of listing things we remember were important to us, or to a particular creative writing project. Then considering where we might draw a line between the internal and external. Nor is considering influences likely to be a case of knowing each nuance of each influence accurately enough that we can be certain what to list and in what ways the influence impacted upon us. However, the act of discovering influences on our creative writing, and in our creative writing, is also the act of understanding what we value or believe to be significant to us and to our writing. It is in that act, the searching and the consideration, that we can make our discoveries.

For example, if we believe our childhood interest in the outdoors influences our writing, in what ways does it do that and to what extent? Does it provide us with subject matter, influence our choice of themes, suggest to us settings, encourage us to go write in certain places? If we are certain that an historical event was influential on our writing decisions, the content of a work we're producing or the themes we explore, what was it about the event that attracted us, and how does our interpretation of it match or challenge the interpretations of others?

In the latter question, we might find that there is a variation in our creative response, where it is presented as imaginative rather than as factual. If we are drawn to a contemporary social issue or to the impact of a new technology or to a particular political situation or to the explorations of a contemporary art form or to a new discovery made by scientists or social scientists, what is it about these things that we find to be influential, and how influential are they?

So, although what influences our creative writing is surely complex, and perhaps never likely to be entirely available to us in all its nuances, we are able to reach toward an understanding. Similarly – while we can label influences 'internal' and some 'external', some from within ourselves, some out in society, some about the imagination, some about the experiences we're having – influences are ultimately integrated and associated, not separated. The following is a list of some areas of influence and how we might best understand them:

Environment

Firstly, the local world in which we write. Secondly, the wider cultural world in which we live. These can be starting points for considering environmental influence. Does the fact you live in the suburbs change what you write about – compared to, say, if you lived downtown, in the middle of the city or in the countryside or out on a farm? Environmental influences, each and all!

We are not beginning here from the idea of a creative work existing, but rather from the point of view of you making it exist. From that point of view, the point of view of a creative writer at work, environmental influence might be identified on a large scale or a small scale, contemporary or historic. Influences on your creative writing can be the result of environmental consistency (that is, something that has remained as it is now for some time) or of environmental change (that is, a writing event that owes its shape and character and, ultimately, its results to a change of circumstance). Russian writer Vladimir Nabokov, writing of his period of exile in England, France and Germany, comments:

> Roots, roots of remembered greenery, roots of memory and pungent plants, roots, in a word, are enabled to traverse long distances by surmounting some obstacles, penetrating others and insinuating themselves into narrow cracks. (Nabokov, 1982: 235)

Roots in this paragraph are clearly not only literal. The interaction of Nabokov and his environment, given the types of influence and exchange he describes ('memory', 'traversing', 'penetrating', 'insinuating'), is fascinating to consider.

If we work for simplicity from your personal space outward, the influences include those of where you write, on what you write and what the specific characteristics of your writing 'space' entail. For example, is your writing usually undertaken in a space of quiet contemplation, a private space, a public space, surrounded by people, a space in which all the resources you need to write are located? Is your personal writing environment separate from your living space or melded with it? What influence does your most personal of environments have on your writing? And, incidentally, environments are also not just physical entities, they are about conditions and influences that involve other people. So, personal influence can also mean the influence of those who are closest to you.

Beginning by considering influences on your personal environment, and your personal environment on your writing, from what it contains to how it is decorated to where it is located, we might then broaden our consideration. Consider the cultural influences of our city or state, compare historical differences, what your environment is like now to what historical evidence impacts, remaining buildings, long-established cultural traditions, common travel routes from one place to another.

Your environment might be 'pro writer', so to speak, in that you experience it as a supportive habitat, surroundings that empower you to write. Or your environment might be 'writer challenging', perhaps not entirely subverting your writerly needs but a source of occasional frustration, something against which you have to push to get your writing done.

Environmental influences can include the contexts of social class and wealth, whether where you live and what you have to do to survive make your creative writing a simple or difficult choice. It can include the circumstances of family, support, obligations, as well as those roles of friends or of colleagues. It can incorporate specific professional advisors, editors, literary agents, critical opinion providers in cognate areas of endeavor, like those who study English literature, or who work in the theater, or produce media, or are fellow creative writers.

Your environmental influences can include the shifting, perhaps seasonal, conditions of work and play, travel and hunkering down at home, the cycles of climate, where your physiological conditions mesh with your psychological states. In this, making it perhaps too cold to write, or too warm to write, or put you in a state of mind where the play of dark on light makes that concentrated play of the imagination with formal intellectual needs of orchestrating the written word exhausting. Or the perfect time to go to the beach and leave writing behind, or an ideal time to simply write all day.

All this is not focused narrowly on the subjects and themes of your writing. Rather, it is related broadly to *where* you write, *how* you write, *when* you write and *for whom* you write. This we can call a responsive approach to what creative writing is – an approach where we are considering the clues that exist about environmental influence on you as a writer and therefore on what occurs during your writing. Of course, these environmental influences can also be a direct, even significant contributor to *what* you write. The texts you produce might indeed contain much evidence of these and other environmental influences, but here in seeking clues the search has included your writerly surroundings, the physical, the mental, the personal, the societal.

Psychology

Why do you write creatively? Would you say it is mostly because of your *want* to write, or is it because of your *need* to write? These two questions alone could help construct an initial framework for making discoveries about why you are a creative writer. However, as with much here, it is not the completeness of your answers that is most significant but the act of asking such questions in the first place. F. Scott Fitzgerald writes:

> The history of my life is the history of the struggle between an overwhelming urge to write and a combination of circumstances bent on keeping me from it. (Phillips, 1988: 107)

and

> I'd rather live on less and preserve the one duty of a sincere writer – to set down life as he sees it as gracefully as he knows how. (Phillips, 1988: 113)

It is perhaps most difficult of all to discover general personal, psychological influences on all your creative writing. Far easier to recall a specific material influence and a specific reaction, say a particular novel and your joy in reading it, as the impetus for your decision to write your own work; or to tie a need to express yourself to a particular social or natural event. The stimuli of instances like these are less difficult to assess. Indeed, though we can relatively easily pinpoint an emotive moment, a memorable sight or someone's poignant comment, we might never map all the interactions of our mind and our experiences, our feelings and our creative writing responses. And yet, even with that proviso, we can still explore some of the characteristics of our mental reactions in order to better consider where the general connections might be. For example:

• *Behaviour*. Considered as the way in which you act as well as how you interact with others, imagine the significance of discovering your behavioral patterns on your understanding of your creative writing. Clues here to how to behave when you're writing – Do you shut yourself away or go out and engage with other people? Do you read constantly? Interview friends about topics you're writing about? Drink more wine, walk more in your neighborhood, spend less time in bed? – reflect on how you develop ideas, what ideas most often attract you, what patterns emerge when you compose your works, how you deal with taking your emotional reactions and using the written word to convey these reactions. Screenwriter Robert Carlock, recalling his writing on TV sitcoms *30 Rock* and *Friends*, as well as his work on *Saturday Night Live*, relates the collaborative nature of the writing, and how groups of writers behaved:

> you're in a room and someone is giving guidance to that room, let's say it's me. So you're saying this is what we're left with at the end of the season, and you want to try and focus on the next step in the larger story. By now hopefully you've broken into these smaller rooms, let's say it's me and four other people, and you just talk it through. Then you put it on the board, and see how it looks like. You look at the outline, then you probably call the other room in and share that with them and make your adjustments. We are used to doing three of four stories for an episode. (Kallas, 2014: 77)

Your behavioral characteristics could involve writing 'mannerisms' – your style choices, your favored words, most likely genre, characters you prefer to write about, rhythms you create, appearance of your writing on the page, even how frequently you complete work and publish it, all could be considered behavioral characteristics personally associated with you.

• *Processes.* Psychology is processes as well as attitudes. Your behavior reflects something of your processing: the way you go about things is defined by how your mind affects your functions. So, behavior is one indication. But processes also involve selecting and ordering, combining, heightening some things and diminishing the importance of others – concepts that are relevant to your writing as well as your everyday life. That is, you prefer more chocolate cake to more French fries so you ensure your kitchen cupboards are stocked with cake mixes but occasionally you forget to buy potatoes – it is also the case that your creative writing will show process preferences, preferences related to the process of telling or showing, informing, entertaining, how you envisage order or image, contrast or parallel viewpoints, adhere to or change tone.

• *Order and disorder* are perceived states and we each live and function within a sense of these. While there are some common-sense agreements about both – for example, we can generally agree on what is disheveled or cluttered – our personal sense of order and disorder is more nuanced, more individual. Because creative writing involves ordering words, and because our sense of ordering is in some part individual, then our sense of order and disorder influences what we write and how. We can speculate, even without researching details, that those writers who began or developed particular literary movements or modes of writing had some agreement with a certain sense of order and disorder. We can speculate also that part of our enjoyment of a particular form of writing, or a particular author's way of writing comes about at least in part because we find something satisfying about the order or, indeed, the disorder contained within this. These are psychological states not solely responses to elements of graphic design or to patterning of story or rhythm, though these can certainly be part of the overall affect.

• *Attitude.* Our settled ways of thinking and feeling are most often regarded as attitudes. While these might change at some point, their longevity, their strength and their embeddedness within our personal psychology make them significant drivers of our actions and reactions. Regardless of how open-minded we believe ourselves to be, we all have these. Attitudes influence our creative writing either because they come to the fore when we are choosing what we write about, what interests us and how we feel about it, or because they impact on how we interpret events or people or colors, beauty, generally, or relationships or feelings – all manner of things and events! French novelist and essayist Marcel Proust, writing in 1898 to Marie Nordlinger, who would later assist him with his translations of work by English art critic John Ruskin, reveals some of his attitudes, in this case initiated by a Christmas card Nordlinger has sent him:

> If we were creatures only of reason, we would not believe in anniversaries, holidays, relics or tombs. But since we are also made up in some part of matter, we like to believe that that too has a certain reality and we want what holds a place in our hearts to have some small place in the world around us and to have its material symbol, as our soul has in our body. (Kolb, 1983: 188)

Because creative writing is an exchange, most often between the one and the many, the writer and an audience, attitudes are an influence not only on what we write but on who responds to what we write. Discovering clues to our attitudes and the attitudes of others is an element in investigating psychological influences on our writing.

• *The psychologies of others.* You might have little knowledge of these, little actual data – but others' personal psychology has the potential to influence your writing. We make assumptions about responses, and endeavor to control them in some way or ways. A common question in creative writing classes is: 'who is your audience?' This question can refer directly and pragmatically to who will buy your work. However, selling your writing might not be your priority, and the question does have a wider meaning. Additionally, since the advent of contemporary digital technologies made the possibility of distributing works of creative writing more freely, to more people, a reality the 'exchange... between the one and the many' might for you be more about what communities of people you are reaching (persons with similar interests in the subjects or themes of your writing) or about the ability to receive feedback for works in progress or about developing an entire alternate persona attached to your creative life.

While perceiving who might respond positively to your work can be an influence on what you write and on how you write, we each might claim different levels of concern with this – dismiss it entirely as an influence on us, or say we write directly and unequivocally for someone or someones. But the psychology of others influences us both in its paralleling our own psychology – so we think of people like ourselves when we are composing our works – and in projecting potentially alto-gether persons, real or imaginary, for whom we write, or whom we incorporate into our works as characters or as owners of viewpoints or as providers of voices. John Gardner alludes to some of this when he says in *The Art of Fiction*:

> all writers, given adequate technique – technique that communi-cates – can stir our interest in their special subject matter, since at heart all fiction treats, directly or indirectly, the same thing: our love for people and the world, our aspirations and fears. The particular characters, actions and settings are merely instances, variations on the universal theme. (Gardner, 1991: 42–43)

Gardner here moving from the general to the particular – the idea that if we are aware of others (and he goes on to talk of writers believing in human free will, in that regard) then we can write from what are widely known themes to what he calls 'specific subject matter'. Both by comparison with others, and by thoughts about ourselves, we include our reasons for writing creatively as part of our sense of identity. Identities being made by comparison, because we can only perceive of ourselves by perceiving how we share similarities and differences with oth-ers, the psychologies of other people (or how we perceive these) are often strong influences on our creative writing.

Time and Space

While we can include a general influence of when we are writing (time) with where we are writing (space) as environ-mental factors, writing is itself a communication medium (and, in the case of creative writing, an art form) that exists and operates in time and space.

Time, in that structures of writing suggest particular chronologies, relationships between one event and another or one observation and another, that have taken place at one time or another. Time, also – in the sense of time taken to compose a piece of work, and time for each element of that writing – time is an ordering force. 'Time', Mario Vargas Llosa suggests, 'is an essential part of fiction that gives it a separate identity, a personality that is different from real reality'.

> For obvious reasons time in a novel is never like time in real life. This is true even in the most realistic novel, in the novel that succeeds in imitating life. In a novel, time always has a beginning and end. It never flows as it does in real life. In a novel, because you have to tell how different characters are acting or moving or thinking, you are obliged to stop in order to differentiate the characters, actions, and episodes. Thus you are forced to break the movement time has in reality, and so you are always introducing an artificial time in a novel. (Llosa, 1991: 97)

It might be that your ability to allocate time is a factor in starting and completing any piece of writing. But consider that while time in its scientific guise can be measured, perceptions of time vary – they vary between cultures and they vary between individuals. We most often live according to shared and agreed scientific agreement on time measurements. Common sense makes this so. But that scientific measurement of time is only some of what time means to us, and those personal interpretations, your sense of time, its dimensions and its impact are persuasive too.

Space, not in this case in terms of location but in terms of the occupation of space by the inscribed word. When you write, you inscribe in a place and take up space. The written word is presented graphically or verbally – so we can see it or hear it in some way, even when it is guiding the production of another art form (such as in the context of a film script or a play). Writing therefore is *in space*, it occupies a spatial position. We see this most sharply when one word is written over another or, in a conversation perhaps, one person speaks over another. When words overlay each other, attempting to be in one space, they often become incomprehensible. Words cannot easily occupy the same space – they vie for significance. We prioritize – through writing convention and, in the wider world, through social convention. The influence of this notion of space – whereby two things (in this case words or collections of words) cannot occupy the same space certainly bears the logic of physics (as anyone who has been involved in a car accident will attest!). As a creative writer, the key concept is about priorities – if creative writing occupies space, fills space, is patterned in space, what are your priorities for using this fact?

Events

Throughout a writer's life, events occur that are influential, though not all these events have the same shape and form, and of course they don't all have the same impact. There are three broad categories of event:

• *Cyclical events*. Events occurring at regular intervals. These events can therefore be predicted, and plans made ahead of them, when needed. Such events as annual holidays and celebrations, personal anniversaries, natural events such as seasonal change, the arrival of morning and evening, political terms that must result in elections. The influence of cyclical events on your creative writing is such as to suggest patterns, and the patterns created by them on your life in general emphasize order and organization. While such an emphasis might be partial, it is interesting to consider how much the order created by cyclical events impacts on our sense of structure and form in general, whether in writing or in life.

• *Regular events*. So, here, while it might be predicted to rain in your local area more often in spring than in autumn, the season itself is 'cyclical', the rain, which arrives less predictably, is 'regular'. Cyclical events happen in the same order, over and over again. Regular events happen over again but not necessarily in the same order; nor, unlike cyclical events, do they always relate back to a common starting point. Regular events influence us also by suggesting patterns, but in this case the formal pattern is less rigid, the occurrences less sure.

• *One-time events*. Sometimes considered as disjunctures or ruptures in a pattern of activity or coming about as the result of planning with a goal in mind, one-time events have the potential to greatly influence us because of their uniqueness. John Barth, though not noting their influence on his own writing, is clearly aware of influential one-time events going on in the world:

> Outside our house, meanwhile, the cold war ended, Germany reunited, the French and British Chunnel-diggers shook hands under the Channel, the new Persian Gulf crisis bade equally (as of this writing) to midwife a new world order or to abort it, and, depending on one's way of counting, either the 1980s ended or the Nineties began. (Barth, 1995: 160)

Because one-time events can sometimes be unexpected, unplanned and even disruptive, their ability to impact on us emotionally can be considerable. Plainly, our birth and death are one-time events, for example! Some events in politics, sports, in popular entertainment, in nature or in the built environment, to name just a few, might be one-time events in our lifetime. We might experience firsts in a particular field, or encounter natural phenomena that we personally will never see again. One-time events, whether planned or fortuitous, focus our attention and, because of their singularity, encourage us to respond. Whether dismissed as anomalies or considered a crossroads, one-time events tend to be notable for us creative writers because inventiveness, newness, is the lifeblood of creative writing. We see the results of this in the way we develop focal points in stories, using exposition, description and dialogue to create events, or in how we create rises and falls in the rhythm of poetry or when we include a complicating action in a film script.

People

Both art and form of communication, creative writing exists between the innovations of the imagination and the relative ordinariness of the written world. Innovation because, of course, creativity involves inventiveness and originality. Ordinariness because the written word needs to transfer meaning between people, forming the basis of communication that most often occurs without the writer present.

The ability to transfer meaning and, simply speaking, make sense is fundamental to almost all written communication. Creative writing does not abandon the role of sense-making, but it favors the influences of the imagination which can make the communication more opaque, or multiplex or non-literal. It is in this zone between meaning and non-meaning that much of the influences of people exist for us as writers.

People often directly influence your creative writing by being potential recipients of your finished work. They influence what you do by your projections of what might best communicate to them, one or many of them – or, indeed, sometimes by how far you might travel away from standardized forms of written communication in the interests of inventiveness, knowing the further your travel from these well-established modes of communication, the more likely it will be that someone will 'not get it'. In that sense, people influence your aesthetic explorations, your stylistic choices, how far you veer from genre conventions, your use of the symbolic and the emblematic, whereby these are widely known within your cultural group. People, of course, also influence the subjects on which you write, and the themes you choose to explore. Bohemian-Austrian poet and novelist Rainer Maria Rilke's *Letters to a Young Poet* is an example of a direct exchange of this kind. Rilke writing back to young poet Franz Kappus, who sought out his advice in the initial years of the 20th century:

> And the point is, to live everything. *Live* the questions now. Perhaps you will then gradually, without noticing it, live along some distant day into the answer, Perhaps you do carry within yourself the possibility of shaping and forming as a particularly happy and pure way of living; train yourself to it – but take whatever comes with great trust, and if only it comes out of your own will, out of some need of your inmost being, take it upon yourself and hate nothing. (Rilke, 1954: 35)

And Kappus writing in his Introduction to the book about the exchange:

> I determined in that very hour to send my poetic attempts to Rainer Marie Rilke and to ask him for his opinion. Not yet twenty, and close on the threshold of a profession which I felt to be entirely contrary to my inclinations, I hoped to find understanding, if in any one, in the poet who had written *Mir zur Feier*. (Rilke, 1954: 12)

Those close to you are likely to provide traits of language or ways of viewing things, whether or not you draw from these consciously. They will offer up opinions with which you agree or disagree and your responses to these can also find their way into your works. They are also likely to be supportive, ambivalent or, perhaps even on occasion, unsupportive of your work as a creative writer. Your sense of purpose and how you feel about your writing can therefore also be influenced by people – and though this is by no means a unique occupational fact, the majority of creative writers do not make their living from writing; therefore, the influence of anyone wondering why you do it at all might well be interesting to consider!

Other Works

A poem you admire inspires you to write a poem of your own. A short story inspires a short story. A novel a novel. Perhaps! Alternatively, there is cross-fertilization: novel to poem, short story to play script, play script to…. Perhaps you have read a magazine article and decided to take the core of it, imagine the report further, develop some creative avenues of inquiry and, from this, write a movie. These are examples, if somewhat simplified examples, of a type of exchange. On occasion, this type of exchange finds its way into college literature classes about writers in a certain period of literary history or who openly wrote about fellow writers whose works they admired. There's no denying this happens. But creative writers are also often audacious readers and active consumers of all manner of information-based and entertainment-based material.

Literary works might indeed influence you. However, so might films you watch and what you read on the internet. You might be influenced by the TV news or by a video you watched online or the mini-series you binge viewed. Scientific works, other art forms, the influence of historical family documents unearthed in cleaning house. The written word is the tool of the creative writer but this doesn't restrict a writer to literature, and certainly not to great works of literature, or only to those works that emerge from the same technically informed or culturally informed camp as our own.

We find value placed on certain forms of completed texts, some of which are works of creative writing. That value is not necessarily misplaced, but it is most likely based on critical opinion of the final work or on the status of the writer of that work (sometimes through reputation as a writer, sometimes because they have popular iconic value for other reasons). None of this, by default, determines that this is or should be influential on you as a writer. The works that influence you, that most inform what you write and why you write and perhaps even how you write can be anything. Amanda Gorman, who in 2018 became the first person to be named National Youth Poet Laureate of the United States, declares:

> I'll never forget being in third grade, and my teacher, Shelly Fredman, a writer in her own right, was reading Ray Bradbury's novel 'Dandelion Wine' to our class. I don't remember what the metaphor was exactly — something about candy — but I lost my mind. It was the best thing I'd ever heard. Pure magic! (*New York Times*, 2018)

You can also write 'to' a work – that is, broadly speaking, by emulation – or 'away from' a work – that is, concertedly in opposition to its style or its interpretations or its aesthetic traits. A number of works might influence one of your projects, and you might pick and combine influences (as always, being unaware of some, and entirely aware of others). Discovering certain kinds of other works exist at all could well be invigorating – the sense that certain projects are possible to complete, that particular types of knowledge exist, or that there is a tradition of writing that spans generations and cultures.

Success and Failure

Any number of gurus of self-help, business success and the wonders of human learning suggest failing at something assists us, eventually, to become successful. How we use failure is the clue. Evidence certainly suggests that how we react to failure has the potential to be more significant to us than the failure itself. Whether we quote the case of the inventor who was aiming to invent one thing but ended up inventing another, or recall how a succession of unsuccessful starts spurred a novelist or an actor, a technologist or a politician on to eventual triumph, success and failure do not appear to be opposites as much as they are points on a continuum. With this in mind, in considering the influences on our creative writing we might well take into account:

What were we aiming to achieve? Success and failure in creative writing are best defined by our own expectations. Personal growth, individual expression, financial gain – none of these are more right as achievements than any other, but any of them could be your primary influencing force. Perhaps you are aiming to achieve more than one thing, equally, or to achieve a great many but in a wide order of importance.

Can your creative writing be both successful and a failure? Absolutely! So, the short story you consider one of your least technically accomplished is selected for publication in a 'Best Short Stories of the Year' series. Or the film script you feel least connected to, personally, is the one picked up for production. The notion of failure here is one of 'not meeting your expectations'. Of course, the opposite can also be true – that something regarded as a failure by others is regarded by you as entirely successful. The sense of success and failure is also only related to material end results. It could be that the success or failure of any event of creative writing is in the event itself – perhaps what is learned during the writing, or explored, or what is shared with others while the writing is happening, or what is unearthed factually or emotionally.

If you feel you succeeded, does this success mean you will repeat the same project in some way? Because creative writing by definition involves creativity, it is with newness, inventiveness and innovation that it is most associated. Even successful works do not therefore always encourage a writer to do similar things, or to undertake a project in exactly the same way. In fact, it can be that a creative writer avoids doing that, regardless of the consequences.

What is your tolerance for failure? If you enjoy creative writing, and you want to achieve something with it that gives you satisfaction, how much energy and time are you willing or able to apply to continuing doing it if you don't get that satisfaction? It is interesting to contemplate how difficult we imagine creative writing to be. Certainly, because it is a respected art, and because culturally we revere those who do it well, there's an inherent suggestion that it *should* be hard and we must endure some kinds of technical, financial, even social hardship to reach our goals. If such a notion influences you, then it might well keep you writing when otherwise you would not. If its influence is to turn a sense of pleasure to a condition of relentless labor then the opposite might be true!

What is your tolerance for success? This might appear a strange question! However, if the challenge of creative writing is one of the drivers of your interest then success is not satisfaction, maybe not even productive. This feeling is not exclusive to what we do as writers. In *An Astronaut's Guide to Life on Earth*, astronaut Chris Hadfield (2015: 100) argues that 'early success is a terrible teacher. You're essentially being rewarded for a lack of preparation, so when you find yourself in a situation where you must prepare, you can't do it. You don't know how'. The influence of success in that respect could be to reduce the chances of a long-term life as a creative writer, or push you to try new techniques, subjects or themes in pursuit of creative energy or highlight something you are doing well when you were unaware of that fact. It might place you in a position of being influential on other writers who look to you for guidance, or draw upon your works for their inspiration, or suspect you know things about creative writing that they do not know — even if you are sure that is not the case!

Examples of influence, as all and any of these happen to be, recall for us the place of the writer in a network of interactions and intersections. Our own identities, formed as they are through nurture as well as nature, are already that kind of thing, an amalgam and a collection, varying over time and holding fast to certain elements as well. Influences on our creative writing, and on what we produce through our creative writing, offer something of a road map to what we think and feel, if we can read these influences well enough. Poet Michael Hamburger, writing in *The Truth of Poetry: Tensions in Modernist Poetry Since Baudelaire*, and quoting Wallace Stevens, comments:

> The poet 'has had immensely to do with giving life to whatever savour it possesses. He has had to do with whatever the imagination and the senses have made of the world'. 'The world about us would be desolate except for the world within us'. (Hamburger, 1996: 104)

As with influences on other parts of our lives, it is the conversation between what appears internal to our personal make up and what appears in the external world that empowers the level and role of influence. Because creative writing involves the shared and shareable structures of writing and the personal fluidity of our imaginations, influences for creative writers are potential explanatory tools to assist us in critically evaluating how our works are coming about, what we value in writing and how any works ultimately look when they are completed.

While we can't control all of what influences us, we can endeavor to locate and understand a great deal of it. Where we can control influences, heightening or lessening them – whether it is by exposure to certain things, or by deeper consideration of what we are doing and why, or by changing our patterns of behavior – opportunities lie to compare and contrast the impact, and to make decisions about our preferences.

References

Barth, J. (1995) *Further Fridays: Essays, Lectures and Other Non-Fiction, 1984–1994*. Boston, MA: Little Brown.

Evans, M. (ed.) (1985) *Black Women Writers: Arguments and Interviews*. London: Pluto.

Gardner, J. (1991) *The Art of Fiction: Notes on Craft for Young Writers*. London: Vintage.

Gass, W. (1986) *Habitations of the Word: Essays*. New York: Touchstone.

Hadfield, C. (2015) *An Astronaut's Guide to Life on Earth: What Going to Space Taught Me About Ingenuity, Determination, and Being Prepared for Anything*. New York: Back Bay.

Hamburger, M. (1996) *The Truth of Poetry: Tensions in Modernist Poetry Since Baudelaire*. London: Anvil.

Kallas, C. (2014) *Inside the Writers' Room: Conversations with American TV Writers*. Basingstoke: Palgrave.

Kolb, P. (1983) *Marcel Proust: Selected Letters, 1880–1903*. Chicago, IL: University of Chicago.

Nabokov, V. (1982) *Speak Memory: An Autobiography Revisited*. Harmondsworth: Penguin.

New York Times (2018) A Young Poet's Inspiration. See https://www.nyt imes.com/2018/02/28/us/a-young-poets-inspiration.html (accessed 12 August 2019).

Phillips, L. (1988) *F. Scott Fitzgerald On Writing*. London: Equation.

Rilke, R.M. (1954) *Letters to a Young Poet* (trans. M.D.H. Norton). New York: Norton.

5 Endings

Much as starting creative writing involves decision-making and taking action to begin, finishing means knowing when you are done. There are also two meanings here: the ending of a piece of work (novel, poem, etc.) and your concluding of your working on it. Here 'ending' is also used as shorthand for 'outcome' and 'result' – though the nuances between these things we can and will also consider.

How do you know when you are finished writing the piece you are working on? What is a successful ending? These are questions that have long been pondered by creative writers, as well as by those who attempt to instruct others about key aspects of creative writing – such as this by science fiction writer Nancy Kress, author of such books as the Hugo and Nebula-winning novella *Beggars in Spain* (1991):

> The most-asked question when someone describes a novel, movie or short story to a friend probably is, 'How does it end?' Endings carry tremendous weight with readers; if they don't like the ending, chances are they'll say they didn't like the work. Failed endings are also the most common problems editors have with submitted works. (Kress, 2008)

Comments such as 'you don't finish a work you abandon it' and 'endings write themselves' refer to a certain mystery that is as much about the art in creative writing as it is about the physical labor or about the physical shape of what we produce. Because the imagination can be speculative and connective, because it can offer alternative scenarios, combine fact with invention, there is a sense that writing approached creatively has no real end. And yet, the simple architecture of the physical objects we create (novels, poems, scripts) tells us that at some point, we stop writing and, at some point, our works are to all intents and purposes complete.

With these things in mind, rather than refer to 'endings' or 'conclusions', we can think here in terms of 'outcomes' because by outcomes you refer to the consequences or to the results of something that you are doing.

An outcome might indeed be a certain ending to a poem or a story. It might be how the final chapter of a novel is shaped so that what has come before feeds into how the reader is brought to sense meaning in the journey to this point. It might be the way in which a film script provides for alternative interpretations, so that individual members of its audience might well have different opinions on what has occurred. It might be the virtual reality experience you create, where the teller is in many senses not you, as the writer, but the user or player. The immersive nature of a virtual reality experience suggests the conclusion of what you have created relates to (a) what agency you have given the 'reader' in the environment you have created; (b) where you limit the field of view (FOV); and (c) whether in fact the 'ending' is more about how long the user is in the environment, how much they are enticed to stay, how many alternate experiences they seek and have – the 'conclusion' in this way being many conclusions rather than one.

Both in terms of the actions of writing and of the texts you produce, a result can only be defined accurately if we know what we're seeking to achieve. At least, that is, a *successful* result can only be defined with that information. If as a writer you are simply seeking to put words on a page and you do that, then your result is achieved – you've reached your conclusion, you have an ending. That is not meant to be a facetious observation, but it is a purposely disingenuous one because as a creative writer you are never simply aiming to put words on a page – any words, in any way. Creative writing is an art *in* writing and *of* writing, applying inventiveness to written language in a way that frequently takes the ordinary and commonplace needed for much written communication and makes it extraordinary, empowered by the imagination and often displaying considerable originality.

Your reasons for undertaking creative writing can be many, and not all of them might relate to a final work that you produce and then aim to see published. In fact, your reasons and expectations might not always include publication or any widespread distribution of your work. Here, the use of creative writing in a university nursing program, with the results not connected with publication:

> The use of creative writing as part of an academic masters-level assignment has encouraged a different form of engagement that should enhance student reflexivity in facilitation. The approach could be incorporated into other aspects where self-awareness is needed and might be a novel approach for developing practice, such as for compiling Nursing and Midwifery Council revalidation evidence [Nursing and Midwifery Council, 2015b]. (Price *et al.*, 2016: 7)

Your results might, alternatively, relate to distributing your work to a small, private group (friends, a writing group to which you belong, your spouse, children or grandchildren). They might be about expressing something creatively in words that you really want to express, just for yourself. They might be about recording something you don't want to forget, and to do so in an imaginative way. In truth, results in creative writing are about what is satisfying to you, the writer. If we turn back to results as endings, the conclusion of your poem or novel or script is likely to be a result that is satisfying to you as well as any audience you might project. This means that to understand results (of all kinds) we can consider such things as:

In general
Why are you seeking to write creatively?
What satisfaction do you get from this activity?
Who is the audience for what you write?
Do you imagine writing the project you're working on, only, or do you imagine (or have you already) seen creative writing become a regular part of your life?
For endings/conclusions
Why is this result appropriate?

For whom is it appropriate?

In what way or ways does this ending satisfy you, as the writer?

Your answers to such questions as these, shape and influence your sense of an ending. Your sense of its result (that is, a consequence or a conclusion) can thus be that overarching reasoning that guides your writing. That reasoning will allow you to determine when you have an ending at all – and, of course, help you determine if that result is successful or unsuccessful. You could be seeking to achieve a number of things, perhaps with varying degrees of significance.

To make discoveries about how we perceive and produce creative writing endings, we are asking ourselves, individually, to determine what motivates us, what keeps us going, what thrills us perhaps, certainly what satisfies us. These are intricate considerations! Yet, plainly, if endings (personal ones or textual ones) reflect a certain viewpoint, then at the very least attempting to better know that viewpoint assists us in determining how we act and the results expected from those actions.

For those who write creatively for any length of time, the personal satisfaction gained from doing so must surely be high – even if, like television dramatist and screenwriter Dennis Potter (speaking here to Graham Fuller), that satisfaction is played down somewhat:

GF: *Do you want to write until you can't write any more?*

DP: I think I'm already at that stage, don't you? I'm about there. It's my job – that's all I can say. I can't imagine what I'd do if I didn't. Writing and what you have to attend to after, like producing – in the way that I believe a producer should be like: getting a thing going and then nourishing and cosseting it, bringing out from it what is in it, with all those people that surround you, and all of *their* people and all of *their* skills. Without that I wouldn't know what to do. There'd be no point. Yes, I will write until something knocks down my hand, I suppose. What that something might be I am not willing to contemplate! (Fuller, 1993: 140–141)

Logically, creative writing must provide a high degree of personal satisfaction for a creative writer, because the majority of us do not make a living from our writing – that is, the majority of creative writers write because they *want* to write not because they *have* to write. If we consider this for a moment, and compare it with other things we do in life, we begin to get some sense of how creative writing results relate to both the engagement of our intellects (the figuring out of what we need to do and applying the tools we have to do it) and our emotions (seeking to do that which will bring us and potentially others gratification). This is the case whether we are talking about creating an ending for a play script or assessing what results we desire from our writing in general. We can summarize endings from several perspectives, as follows:

Personal

The endings of our work, or the results, we can define according to pleasure or pride, contentment, satisfaction or fulfillment. It might be simply completing that poem you are working on that brings you the result you have been seeking. Whether others enjoy that poem, or whether it means anything to anyone but you might be of little real importance. Similarly, it could be that seeing your novel published by a well-known press is a considerable point of pride for you. These are personal results, defined largely by you rather than by others.

If we acknowledge that creative writing (the doing and the receiving of it, equally) involves our emotions as well as the capacity to intelligently read and interpret, then it stands to reason that personal results (whether individual or group) are connected to our feelings and influenced by our individual psychology. With that in mind, an end goal for you as a writer might be sharing your work with family or friends, because in doing so you are connecting more deeply with them. This could take the form of offering stories or observations that you feel cannot effectively be offered in any other way. It could be to enable the recording of elements of family history, creatively, or endeavoring to reveal to those you love your feelings or thoughts.

Results in creative writing are also influenced by the societies in which we live, and sometimes those outcomes can have cultural and societal significance. Outcomes defined here as results that have more enduring or wider-ranging consequences. Where literature is valued (and in a great many societies it is valued), being a creative writer is associated with a vibrant arts sector, and can even be considered to represent the existence of a mature and civil community. Personal outcomes can, in this sense, mean group outcomes – such things as the presence of a regularly renewing literary culture, where new works emerge and contribute to positive social interactions and to education and to discussion and debate. This along with the existence of open dialogue in the media, the performing arts, so that creative writing forms part of a spectrum of empowering exchanges.

Professional

The obvious reference here is to the writer paid to be a writer. In that case, a professional result would clearly be the work or works you are required to write for your job. The success or lack of success of that outcome would relate to whether those works turn out to be fit for purpose – delivered by you as the genre fiction writer, the screenwriter for indie cinema, the writer of scripts for leisure software, the lyricist....

Here, from screenwriter Caroline Thompson, responsible for such films as *Edward Scissorhands* (1990) and *The Nightmare Before Christmas* (1993):

> I had one really good piece of advice, which is don't give yourself X number of years in which to make it. There is no timeline. Lots of people I know said, 'I will give it three years, and if it hasn't worked out by then, I'll go back to doing whatever I was doing before'.
>
> But this friend, the one with the good advice, said to me, 'Just be there. No one can kick you out. Just be there. Stand there long enough and your turn will come around'. And it did. It worked out. (Morgan & Perez, 2013: 178)

We can map each professional role onto the expectations of the industries for which the writer works. We can also consider how works of creative writing conclude and whether that has a relevance to the expectations of the industry in which they work. In general, a successful outcome for you, if you're a professional writer, is the satisfaction of the readers or audiences for whom your works are intended, resulting of course in sales of those works. Further success can be measured by the likelihood that these audiences will expand, that they will pay to experience future works and that the investment made in employing you or contracting you will be more than repaid in profit. In this way, a basic financially determined professional result! However, by professional result we could also mean a number of other things:

• *In education.* Creative writing is frequently incorporated into literacy learning, from the earliest days of education, and in relation to both writing and reading. Results here include general competencies, more than they might relate to aesthetically pleasing results. Because creative writing allows for a wide range of forms and encourages the use of language in both ordinary and extraordinary ways, it can be used as a tool to extend knowledge of how writing works, or to ignite a passion for the joys of reading, or to identify the cultural influences on literacy.

In addition to this wider educational use, creative writing is a well-established discipline in higher education, and results here are not necessarily those related to publication or production. So, a university student might complete a class where the result is the learning of a particular technique, or the developing of a process, or the identification of genre characteristics and the practicing of those. Learning outcomes can be defined by expectations within an entire program of study, so here the aim can be to relate one result to another, some purely knowledge based (such as in the studying of a period of literary history), some perhaps about the application of that knowledge to creating a finished work (such as we frequently see in the college creative writing workshop).

Lastly, faculty working in higher education – worldwide – are often asked to produce creative works, and sometimes are encouraged to produce scholarly works, as contractual aspects of their job. In some countries, the creative writer on campus might be required to continue to produce creative works – and that alone. In other cases, writers are also asked to engage in critical or pedagogic scholarship of some kind, which contributes to the research objectives of the institution. Differing views of creative writing education influence these expectations. In the United Kingdom and Australia, for example, the idea of researching in and through creative writing is well established. For example, creative writing can be submitted in the UK's national system of assessing quality in university research, the Research Excellence Framework (REF); the following from the 2021 assessment and from 'Main Panel D: Arts and Humanities':

> Research outputs that demonstrate originality may do one or more of the following: produce and interpret new empirical findings or new material; engage with new and/or complex problems; develop innovative research methods, methodologies and analytical techniques; *show imaginative and creative scope*; provide new arguments and/or *new forms of expression*, formal innovations, interpretations and/or insights; collect and engage with novel types of data; and/or advance theory or the analysis of doctrine, policy or practice, and new forms of expression. [my italics] (Research Excellence Framework)

and can include among other things:

> creative writing and practice; life writing; ... creative non-fiction and/or creative critical writing. (Research Excellence Framework)

with submissions able to be, in addition to books:

- a creative writing collection (a number of related works that were published in forms other than a book length collection)
- a collection of creative and/or critical work (e.g. related articles, books, choreographic materials, essays, dramaturgical works, films, recordings etc.) on a related topic that address different aspects of a single project and are collectively greater than the sum of their parts. (Research Excellence Framework)

Assessment of such submissions can feature:

> outputs that will meet the REF definition of research as 'a process of investigation, leading to new insights effectively shared' without the need for additional information, and *these may include examples of creative practice.*
>
> *Generating new ways of thinking that influence creative practice*, its artistic quality or its audience reach. [my italics] (Research Excellence Framework)

'The entirety of the material submitted... should provide the panel with coherent evidence of the research dimensions of the work in terms of':

- the research process – the question and/or issues being explored, the process of discovery, methods and/or methodologies, *the creative and/or intellectual context* or literature review upon which the work draws, or challenges or critiques
- the research insights – the findings, discoveries *or creative outcomes of that process.* [my italics] (Research Excellence Framework)

The REF criteria are quoted at length to show the strength of incorporation into ideas of university research. This formal recognition of creative writing as a 'research output' in the United Kingdom (with similar recognition in such countries as Australia), in addition to critical work about creative writing, has long influenced what is considered a professional result for a writer working in British higher education. In the USA, while the growth of 'creative writing studies' as a defined critically focused field has been more prominent recently, many of those employed on US campuses to teach creative writing are primarily expected to produce creative works, and these are not discussed as research in quite the same formal way as we see in the UK's REF.

In all global higher education cases, though, while results from teachers in higher education are not necessarily expected to be commercial, they do come with expectations in regard to such things as the quality of the press that publishes a work, or that such works are well reviewed, or that the authors play some role in using their own writing activities to support a vibrant campus literary climate.

Further, in the 21st century the word 'impact' has been used as a measure of the outcomes of academic research, and creative writing activities have been incorporated into such measurements. So, a collection of poetry by a professor that is published by a well-respected press and that receives good reviews, that is perhaps selected for a literary award and where the professor is invited to read in various venues because of that work, would be described as a result having 'high impact'.

• *Therapeutic uses.* With its combination of the imaginative, emotional and personal, creative writing (like other arts practices too, of course) is regularly used in therapeutic situations. The results here can have relatively little to do with whether a work produced is distributed to other people, or has innate literary merit, or even if it is completed at all. The results of therapy are judged on such things as changes in behavior, or the addressing of symptoms or general improvements in quality of life. Using creative writing therapeutically has a long history – this from an article entitled 'Creative Writing for Therapy' published in *The Elementary English Review* in 1945:

> Every once in a while I let the children take the lid off their kettle. We write about things that have embarrassed us or have made us feel that we're not as good as other people. Then the children gather round while I read their stories out loud to the group. If it is something they don't want others to hear they write 'Just for Mrs. Cole'. (Cole, 1945: 124)

When using creative writing as a therapy, the doing of it could well be heightened to the point where what is produced is not even considered and certainly not assessed. Process can be the sole focus. Alternatively, or additionally, creative writing can be used as encouragement for social interaction – the getting together of a group that writes and shares work, providing support more than providing instruction on how to write. Self-worth, identity, emotional stability can all be part of the evaluation of success here. Clinical results of creative writing in therapy can be formally measured, and there is an established tradition of arts therapies into which these practices fall. Alternatively, informal results for a variety of populations are common – the aged, the socially and economically vulnerable, those recovering from medical or emotional trauma. Interestingly, because writing is part of early literacy education, the familiarity of creative writing to many people might well make it one of the most accessible of arts therapies.

• *Writing in the community*. Storytelling, descriptive or dramatic celebrations of events, highlighting of notable features of daily life, observations on strengths and weaknesses, comments on who we are and why we are and what we do – writing in the community is a term used for a considerable range of practices. Regardless of the diversity of the population, communities are, in fact, defined by common interests and common goals. Being able to express these, define how individuals in the community see their place and their individual and group role and explore how the community defines their lives, these are part of what we often refer to as 'writing in the community'. Incorporating a sense of responsibility for the health and progress of the community, the traditions and the aspirations, writing can work as a mnemonic, reminding us of beliefs and attitudes, strengthening bonds of understanding.

Writing also produces a sense of durability, the recording of things and events and people in a way that suggests they have lasting significance – and when we are doing that using both our imagination and our intellect, we additionally recognize that our emotional landscape is also part of the community, a revelation not always common when we tell our stories according to economic or geographic criterion.

• *Collaborative results (working with others in other fields)*. With its ability to engage diverse groups, and our writerly tendency to draw on knowledge from areas well beyond writing technique, creative writing is used to engage participants in many fields of endeavor. Whether it is the social history of a town or plotting the lives of a population that lives along a certain ancient river, whether it's scientists using creative writing to explore the beauty and personal meaning of the discoveries they have made, or architects using creative writing to involve future occupants of a neighborhood in the personal contexts of their design; whether it begins with the creativity of mathematics and the mathematics of meter or the calculations inherent in literary structure, working collaboratively is an extension of the communicative role of creative writing. What qualifies as an end result here could well be how we are able to share perspectives, combine knowledge to gain even greater knowledge. This from H. Kay Reid and Glenn McGlathery, among many other books and articles devoted to educational exchanges between creative writing and science and/or mathematics:

> Creative writing can (also) be a way to review science. While discussing the writing assignment with the children, question them on how something happens in nature.
>
> Creative writing can (also) be used to introduce a science concept by discussing the story later and comparing the science ideas included to factual information. The children enjoy talking about their stories and why their zany ideas don't occur in our 'neat and orderly' world. (Reid & McGlathery, 1977: 19)

Your Experiences

It is not always that we celebrate the experiences of creative writing over the final results of those experiences. As writers, we are often asked 'what have you written?' but much less so 'what qualities do you value in writing creatively?' Even with the many ways in which creative writing can be used for personal expression, for community engagement, for therapeutic purposes and in education, it is to the artefacts of creative writing that society most often turns to define our results. These material results represent a tangible contribution to the economy.

In the modern world, as job roles became more defined by industrial categories, associated with a growing mercantile economy, having a job with a title and a tangible result matched the modern preoccupation with modes of production and types of consumption. We write, we produce, someone consumes what we write, we produce some more. The economic engine is fueled and a contribution is recognized. Interestingly, in the 21st century we might think of such relatively new occupations as 'social media influencer' and ponder whether intangibility is entering a new phase of economic and societal worth. Regardless, it has always been true that a creative writer's experience of writing only partially relates to the material results and much more connects to the personal, transcendental value in doing it.

Many of the experiences that inform and support our writing results might not be exclusive to creative writing, but they do occupy a unique position in being the result of us working creatively with words. That is one of our most obvious results – the expressing of something creatively, inventively, imaginatively in words when words are so often used in an ordinary way, a way that communicates but does not excite or that informs but ardently does not ask us to think further. Written words are many times used to declare and to explain, to analyze and to directly and as clearly as possible transfer meaning, but in creative writing all that can be beside the point. One aspect of a successful experiential result of your writing might well be the creative use of words.

> But already, we're off to a bad start! These words you are now reading, whose are they? Whose is that voice in your head? Yours or mine? When you hear someone speak, the words remain theirs – to be ignored or disagreed with as you choose. But somehow to read someone's thoughts is to allow them, however temporarily, to take over the language centres of your brain. For as long as you are caught up in what they say, the writer becomes your inner voice. (Cohen, 2011: 3)

As a writer, you're using words to share thoughts and feelings with us. This doesn't only happen in creative writing, but the choices, the modes of expression, they're all enhanced here. Creative writing also has an aesthetic attitude – the pursuit of beauty, which is often colloquially seen to be part of some writing forms (poetry, for example) more than others (a film script, for example). The pursuit of beauty carries with it a sense of virtue in that we have long connected these two ideals, and associated them with such things as harmony, and even with profundity and morality. Questions about these assumptions aside, our result of writing creatively could be a sense of engaging in a noble tradition, a tradition associated with high ideals and purposes.

More pragmatically perhaps, writing involves physical action and the result of deciding to do some creative writing is that you are engaging in a physical activity. It might not be running a marathon or climbing a mountain, but the physical labor of writing combines with the intellectual and creative labor. There is additionally the sense of purpose and accomplishment, given both the actual and perceived labor involved in completing some writing. Perceived because while it might be true that some writing takes time, involves multiple drafts, a substantial length of time and amount of effort, at other times writing simply does not. Cultural value attaches itself particularly to the creation of literature, and in doing so we see assumptions at times about how such valued work gets done. More accurately, the amount of labor varies, as of course does the value assigned to different types of writing and the results of that writing. Even today, despite a long history, the screenplay is not quite regarded as having the same sense of labored refinement as the collection of poetry or the work of literary fiction.

Finally, creative writing combines the two experiences of (a) structuring, because writing must structure communication in order for it to make sense and (b) heightened use of your imagination. Structuring brings order to disordered experience, or gives the impression of doing so. It encourages you to see connections, consider how these inform your own outlook, and to put experiences in context. Expressing yourself in creative writing can therefore be familiarizing, or it can provide you with an outlet for anxiety about why things happen or what things are; or in its ordering of events and ideas, it can provide the comfort found in feeling more sure of things. It is the combined power of making sense but allowing ourselves to employ our imaginative resources, resources we possess beyond our intellects, that enhances the experience of creative writing. No matter why we do it, whether for purely personal satisfaction, for a job or because we use it to engage with other people in some way, the experiences of creative writing are often associated with our sense of identity, with our relationships with others and with us using the relatively ordinary in extraordinary ways.

An ending can be defined as a final part of something – whether that something is the doing of creative writing or whether that ending is the words put on a page or screen as a conclusion. Endings produce results, or effects – whether these are on the reader or audience or on the writer who has finished the work, both working and work now concluded. An outcome, for the purposes of considering endings, I am defining here as something that follows because we have done something, because something has happened. In this case, referring specifically to the 'outcomes' of your creative writing. These might be your enduring personal engagement in a creative life – of which you writing is a primary element. They might be your contributions to a literary, educational or familial culture. They might be your contributions to the world's, the nation's, the region's, your neighborhood's storehouse of stories, histories, observations, exchanges of feeling. Endings might indeed be conclusions – in terms of where a piece of writing stops or a writer 'puts down their pen'. But in how we discover and apply our sense of an ending, endings might well mean us mapping out what gives us satisfaction, how others might react to the work we've produced and what expectations are shared between ourselves and others.

References

Cohen, M. (2011) *Mind Games: 31 Days to Rediscover Your Brain.* Oxford: Wiley.

Cole, N. (1945) Creative writing for therapy. *The Elementary English Review* 22 (4), 124–126.

Fuller, G. (1993) *Potter on Potter.* London: Faber.

Kress, N. (2008) How to Write Successful Endings. See https://www.writersdigest.com/writing-articles/by-writing-goal/improve-my-writing/how_to_write_successful_endings (accessed 12 August 2019).

Morgan, B. and Perez, M. (2013) *On Story: Screenwriters and Their Craft.* Austin, TX: University of Texas.

Price, A., Hirter, K., Lippiatt, C. and O'Neill, K. (2016) Using creative writing to explore facilitation skills in practice. *International Practice Development Journal* 6 (1), 1–9.

Reid, H.K. and McGlathery, G. (1977) Science and creative writing. *Science and Children* 14 (4), 19–20.

Research Excellence Framework. Panel Criteria and Working Methods. See https://www.ref.ac.uk/publications/panel-criteria-and-working-methods-201902/ (accessed 13 August 2019).

Conclusion

Making Your Discoveries

Types of Discovery

This, as you might indeed have noticed, is a book about discovery! Discoveries concerning beginnings, concerning structuring your work. Discoveries about movement, flow and process. Discoveries about the influences on your work. Discoveries with regard to endings.

To make discoveries we seek clues – in this case, clues in and about creative writing – to lead us toward (hopefully!) valid conclusions. So here at the Conclusion, that is essentially what we need to know, and how we need to proceed, to make discoveries about our creative writing (and, generally, about other creative writing too). And then to use those discoveries to reach our goals – *your* goals, whatever your goals might be. Finally, in order to seek clues, we need to know what a clue is, and how then we might use it to find something out.

Generally speaking, a clue is an indicator, a potential guide to your actions that in essence informs your understanding. Other words and concepts associated with 'clues' include such synonyms as 'indications', 'suggestions', 'solutions', 'proof', 'traces' and 'pointers'. So speaking of a 'clue' is shorthand for speaking about evidence to what has happened, is happening or could happen. Clues to your creative writing and in your creative writing are no different. Discover the clues, correctly interpret them and you will learn the things you need to learn to achieve what you wish to achieve. This involves, firstly, finding the evidence and, secondly, having methods to consider it.

When detectives seek clues, they look not only to consider an individual piece of evidence but also to build up a case based on intersecting and interconnecting pieces of information. The stronger and greater the sense of how a clue supports a conclusion, the more valuable that clue becomes; however, each clue, minor or major, forms part of the network of information, and each can potentially assist in creating a fuller and more accurate picture of what has happened or, sometimes, could happen.

When researchers in any field – the sciences, the social sciences, the arts – seek to make discoveries, they often approach this via hypotheses and theories, keeping in mind what they believe happened or what they surmise is correct, and then testing this against the clues, against the evidence they find. A hypothesis in this sense can be confirmed, and thereafter used to assist us in creating or confirming a theory. Theories about things that happen, actions that influence things that happen, theories about objects and about phenomena that we observe, all assist us in modelling our actions and being more confident in how we act and what we can expect from those actions.

In creative writing, clues are both individual (those that relate to your own writing) and general (relating to creative writing as a practice and in relation to its outcomes). In seeking out such clues, often we are aiming to increase our knowledge of how we personally go about doing our creative writing, and what the results can be from those things that we do. We are doing this in order to improve our creative writing, or to assess why a project might not have quite turned out exactly the way we wanted, or to bolster ourselves for undertaking a new project that will challenge our creative skills and our critical understanding of how we write. I have referred to this elsewhere as 'situational knowledge'[1] because it is knowledge we seek in order to address a creative writing situation we face. Situational knowledge therefore occurs like this:

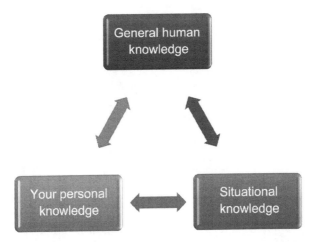

Seeking personal knowledge when creative writing does not mean a creative writer is disinterested in knowing about creative writing more generally, or that they are ambivalent about the situations faced by other creative writers. Simply, like the Formula One driver seeking to know why they failed to navigate a recent curve at the optimum speed, in order to get it right as they approach the next one, or the ballet dancer who landed awkwardly on the last leap and wants to avoid doing so on the next one, or the chemist who miscalculated a gas volume, or the medievalist who interpreted a line of ancient text but realizes in the wider context of the work that other interpretations might be possible, we creative writers are always seeking clues to what we do, so that we can get it right, and so that we might further explore our practice.

Seeking clues to situational knowledge is therefore a fundamental part of creative writing; and it is in this knowledge, and the clues that support it, that our primary interest is often located. But creative writers – not all, perhaps, but a reasonable percentage; certainly all of those who are engaged in the study of creative writing in higher education, for example – also seek to know something more about creative writing in a wider context. Perhaps this is because we feel we might draw from a general principle to our specific needs (that is, from general creative writing knowledge to personal situational knowledge). Or we are naturally inquisitive about how other creative writers work, much as any occupational group has a professional interest in the work of their group members. Or perhaps we read a work or see or hear a work of creative writing and are particularly taken by it, admire the artistry behind it, and therefore seek out clues to how it came about. Clues to creative writing are thus not only sought out on the basis of their individual and perhaps immediate application; sometimes, clues to creative writing are sought with the aim of advancing shared human knowledge about creative writing, of coming to some conclusions about creative writing wherever it occurs and whoever might be doing it.

In some cases, this kind of knowledge is used in the teaching of creative writing – so the clues sought out are both about our own work and about some seemingly customary, frequent and empirically determined discovery we have made, providing a usable insight that we can pass on as teachers to students of creative writing. In other cases, clues to wider or general knowledge about creative writing are sought to situate creative writing in the context of other arts practices. Or to compare it with other forms of writing. Or in order to approach literary, media or performance texts from the point of view of their origins and evolution. Or to consider what aspects of invention, imagination and newness are generated and enveloped in this form of written expression. Or in order to consider the emotional, transcendental or empathetic use of words, and more.

In either case – that of situational knowledge or that of general knowledge – clues to creative writing provide evidence, increase our knowledge and offer a guide to our own creative writing and to creative writing as it is created by others. We can categorize clues along many lines with many focuses. What follows are some examples of evidence we can consider in our seeking out clues to creative writing.

Clues to creative writing can come in the form of *words and numbers* (recalling that when we are talking about clues, we are, synonymously, talking about indications, suggestions, solutions, proof, traces and pointers). A discussion of words you no doubt expected, given that we are talking about writing and, without words, writing would clearly be impossible! Numbers, however, might be a surprise.

The suggestion here is not that creative writing can be reduced to arithmetic and calculations, but that writing involves patterns. It involves observable lengths, shapes, lines, sequences, geometry and topology. It involves diminution and augmentation. In some cases, there are definite numerical guidelines to writing that suggest structure and form, say in the case of formal verse, with its strict meter. In other cases, there is a general sense of length or shape or graphic presentation that is informed by cultural notions of what a particular genre or form of writing entails.

In creative writing, a novel is seen to be longer than a novella; a collection of poetry can be 20–50 pages, rarely shorter or longer; a screenplay has a definite graphic appearance on the page. More generally in writing, a paragraph can be long, short, change length and internal shape (be simple, compound, complex) according to the pace sought or the focus needed. The rhythm of a play or poem or even of a business report or an instruction manual can be determined by the resonance of words and phrases, repeating in measurable beats to attract attention or create a sense of movement or even create physiological connections in this rhythmic expression…. The list could go on, because writing is physical inscription, even when it is figuratively so on a screen, and therefore it manifests in quantities as well as qualities, in proportions and sizes, in measures and in magnitudes.

In essence, then, words make up the majority of what we refer to as 'writing'; but words along with numbers are also organizing principles. As organizing principles, words (or more specifically clues found in word choice, word use, arrangement, relationships created, one word to another, groups of words to other groups) and numbers (or more specifically patterns, lengths, sequences) can be investigated, mined for clues, discussed and, ultimately, the knowledge discovered can be developed and applied.

Creative writing clues can be *literal* and/or *figurative*. A clue acts as a signpost potentially pointing toward a conclusion, toward a truth about something; a clue is evidence that can be used to gain understanding. Clues also relate to one another, so that though they may vary in relevance and significance, they only do so comparatively not independently – and such comparisons are based on how much information, how much knowledge, any clue potentially provides. Some of this information and some of this comparative work might well not exist only (or even at all) on the literal plain of reference. For example, consider a short story you are writing that doesn't appear to be quite reaching your expectations. Literally, the structure, characters, theme, subject, plot all appear entirely viable. But the clue to the story's success is its figurative relationship with rhythm and rhythm's relationship with structural choices, and the 'voices' of the character and that technical aspect's relationship with authority and with believability and with empathy. The literal aspects of constructing the story need the figurative association with melody and resonance. The clues to the success or failure of this short story lie on two planes – one that is represented by how it 'appears' and another by how it 'sounds', the first literal, the second figurative.

Creative writing clues can also be *contextual*. A contextual clue is one that places an action you undertake or a work you are creating or the techniques you are using or the content, or all of this, in relation to something happening, that has happened, that exists or that did exist, something cultural or historical or personal that flags up some aspect of the creative writing, some specific information. Obvious examples would be novels or poems about war written by former military personnel. The context here is not only in terms of the personal experience, but also in terms of the historical facts, the political circumstances. But the context could also influence structure and chosen genre and then the clues discovered *to* the creative writing and, indeed, *in* the creative writing could well relate to how the personal and the public history is used to suggest veracity or to engage the reader in a shared human experience or to challenge perceived opinion about the experiences depicted, because context, historical context for one thing, has foregrounded the story and allowed the writer the opportunity to ground their exploration.

Creative writing clues can be *descriptive* – that is, in an interpretative sense, we might describe a draft of a poem in a certain way. So, the poem is 'pacey' or 'energetic', or it is 'measured', or it is 'contemplative', or it is 'delicate' or 'arousing'. In these descriptions, we are looking to define a feeling, a response, drawing on a combination of our intellect and our emotions. In doing so, and certainly only from our single point of view, we are using description to attempt to capture what we might call 'the essence of the thing'. That is, to respond to that written text (incomplete, that it might be; or, when it is in its final state) in a way that seems to us accurate. In doing so, we have the capacity to ask ourselves if this is the response we want – if it is not, how might we go about adjusting it?

Descriptive clues also come in the form of the formal choices we make. For example, if we choose to write a screenplay and not a poem, our first descriptive clue might come from considering how our script references the nature of film (that is, the use of camera angles, set design, continuity, sound). The descriptive word 'filmic' might encapsulate that investigation; but within it might be clues to the relationship between scenic material and dialogue, between setting and action and so on. In seeking 'the essence of the thing', we're relating a holistic choice of form to individual choices within that creating of a form. Maybe the work should have been a poem not a screenplay – but we will not know that without knowing how to find clues to the success (or lack of success) of our drafts. As well as how to consider our own responses to those drafts (in terms of descriptive clues), how to look at the sequence and rhythm and shape of the film being written, and how to put this in the context of theme and subject and viewpoint. All so that clues to how to write the film (or whether to write a film or a poem or a novel, for that matter) will lie in our ability to identify (a) what represents a clue; (b) how relevant that clue is to the questions we're asking about the work; (c) how significant our discovery is considered to be to our satisfaction with the work; and (d) our capability of acting on what the clues we find lead us to discover.

Methods of Discovery

There are many categories of clues; those above are just some of them. Categorizing evidence of our writing practices and material evidence (such things as drafts, research materials, final results) gives us an opportunity to organize and advance our analysis and therefore our knowledge. All clues have the potential to guide us toward knowledge – *if* we can spot them, *if* we have the tools and methods to analyze them and *if* we are able to interpret them correctly in terms of their relevance and significance.

Creative writing clues, acting as signposts, assist our assessments of the creative writing we have undertaken or are undertaking – and where they are sought out during our writing, rather than when we might believe a work to be complete, we can act on them in motion, resulting in drafts that are closer to our imagined results, often earlier, and therefore saving both time and energy. Creative writing clues, identified either within the text or within your many actions of writing, have the potential to strengthen your creative writing abilities, as well as to provide you with greater understanding, because it is in defining what appears to offer clues to our writing that we build our strengths of observation, interpretation and assessment. In doing so, we potentially make fewer compositional mistakes, gain the ability to hone techniques that can respond to the clues we have found, and become more confident in our writerly actions. The main ways of finding clues (meaning also indications, suggestions, solutions, proof, traces and pointers) in order to make discoveries can be summarized as:

Observation – recall the observed practices of creative writers, and investigate variations on those actions. Include here reflections on how your creative writing appears to come about, the actions of other writers, the many influences on them and circumstances surrounding them and the results of those creative writing actions.

Analysis – examine meanings that can be attached to the creative writer's actions. Analyze and suggest what proof exists to understand creative writing practices, both individual actions and actions interacting with other actions, and the cumulative effect. Analyze how those creative writing actions leave traces in our cultures, as well as in the kinds of work that creative writers produce.

Application – apply what is discovered and what analytical conclusions are reached to investigating and understanding our own, individual creative writing. Take action to use this understanding to advance our own work, providing tools for how we can approach creative writing challenges, address any creative writing problems and complete our works of creative writing.

Results of Discovery

The yearning for knowledge about creative writing and an assumption that if you are a creative writer, or want to be one, you seek understanding of your own creative writing, of the elements of your drafting, the individual projects you undertake and the wider context of your work, informs this book. Simply, that if you are reading here you want to further understand how creative writing is done. Three statements sum up how to achieve this:

(1) We creative writers can undertake investigations of creative writing through our practice of creative writing (what is most often referred to as 'practice-led research') as long as we are aware of the range of clues that appear in and through creative writing, and the ways we might interpret these. Ideally, of course, how we can use the results of our investigations, for beginnings, for structuring, for creating movement, perhaps determining our process, for considering influences and for concluding our work.

(2) Critical analysis of creative writing practice can be undertaken by creative writers or non-creative writers. The purpose of such analysis for those who are not creative writers might be general interest or it might be for academic purposes (such as informing their interpretation of a completed novel or poem). Further, shared situational knowledge discovered in writing practice can inform the personal knowledge of any researcher, as well as adding to the store of human awareness. That said, the majority of

those undertaking such practice-focused analyses are creative writers – simply because we most often seek to apply the results to our own writing.

(3) An individual writer's ability to identify creative writing clues – clues to what you are doing and why you are doing it – can further inform the general public. With attention to this, we each improve the ability of readers and audiences to engage with how creative writing happens and with the considerable variety and intention of creative writing works they encounter. While it might not be necessary to know how to do something to appreciate the results of someone having done it, practice knowledge adds to cultural competence, enabling someone not just to consider creative writing and its outcomes, but also the practices and results of arts and human communication generally. Cultural competence assists in creating empathy, building community, improving communication, clarifying expectations and attitudes and using the power of 'more than one mind'.[2]

To know what modes of investigation we best employ to discover clues and to understand those clues, what methods will best support our investigations and to project the outcomes we can achieve, it is logical first to seek to define what it is we are trying to discover. This is not fixed, of course; but as we seek to know more (if, of course, we do seek to know more!), we have in mind things we'd like to know and we can seek out clues and consider what methods we can use to employ our discoveries – even if at any one time and in any one circumstance our investigations and our reasons for doing them are multiple.

Propelled by your personal aspirations, informed by what you already know about creative writing, associated with the topic or topics of your writing, and linked to acquiring situational knowledge that will help you achieve the results you want, your sense of what you're trying to discover is potentially complex and multilayered – but it is most certainly reachable. For example, is it mostly a technical issue you are considering, something about methods of writing, language use, sentence structure? What clues can assist you with this – clues to what you are doing, what you have done (say in a previous work of creative writing or in your drafting of this one, so far) and clues related to, say, works (complete, incomplete, primary end results or connected results like writers' correspondence or notebooks or diaries) that reveal something of the technical aspects of creative writing, about a particular technical aspect you're considering? Is your question a question about the content of the work, something to do with facts you are using, or to do with how you might associate observations with emotions? What clues assist you here: is there evidence of how content informs creative writing structure or how particular well-known events are interpreted culturally, historically, or how particular emotions impact physical actions, expression, reasoning? Is your investigation of creative writing related to a particular genre, common genre themes? So your clues are potentially contextual – how you, others, interpret those genre codes and conventions. Is your primary focus to look for clues to why the current draft of your short story doesn't appeal to you, or to others, even though it seems well written, and is thus your investigation, your desire for discovery, linked to finding clues about ordering of events or character creation or types of settings or...? And, of course, you might have secondary motivations, a range of additional or even peripheral needs, desires, reasons for wanting to find certain clues, undertake certain investigations and seek to come up with certain results.

Like any investigation, the clues that are found, the ways in which these support or challenge other discoveries and the ultimate results of the undertaking are not always predictable. Nevertheless, some are. Either way, we can seek out clues to our creative writing knowing that we can and will *always* enhance our knowledge – and that, in every instance for the creative writer, the more clues we can identify, the better we are at interpreting these clues, and most often the more skilled we are at applying our new knowledge, the more successful we will be at creative writing.

Notes

(1) Harper, G. (2013) Creative writing research. In G. Harper (ed.) *A Companion to Creative Writing* (p. 284). Oxford: Wiley-Blackwell.

(2) David Kelley, founder of the well-known design company, IDEO, talks about the idea of 'more than one mind', that is one mind building on another, in his interview with '60 Minutes' on CBS in 2013. See https://www.cbsnews.com/news/how-to-design-breakthrough-inventions-07-01-2013/ (accessed 26 August 2019). David and Tom Kelley's book *Creative Confidence: Unleashing the Creative Potential Within Us All*, New York: Crown, 2013, offers some further thoughts on how we all can access, celebrate and enhance our creativity.

Index